Louis Malle

Published in our
centenary year
~ **2004** ~
MANCHESTER
UNIVERSITY
PRESS

Louis Malle

HUGO FREY

Manchester University Press
MANCHESTER AND NEW YORK

distributed exclusively in the USA by Palgrave

The right of Hugo Frey to be identified as the author of this work
has been asserted by him in accordance with the Copyright,
Designs and Patents Act 1988.

Published by Manchester University Press
Oxford Road, Manchester M13 9NR, UK
and Room 400, 175 Fifth Avenue, New York, NY 10010, USA
www.manchesteruniversitypress.co.uk

Distributed exclusively in the USA by
Palgrave, 175 Fifth Avenue, New York, NY 10010, USA

Distributed exclusively in Canada by
UBC Press, University of British Columbia, 2029 West Mall, Vancouver,
BC, Canada V6T 1Z2

British Library Cataloguing-in-Publication Data
A catalogue record for this book is available from the British Library

Library of Congress Cataloging-in-Publication Data applied for

ISBN 0 7190 6456 2 *hardback*
　　 0 7190 6457 0 *paperback*

First published 2004

13 12 11 10 09 08 07 06 05 04   10 9 8 7 6 5 4 3 2 1

Typeset in Scala with Meta display
by Koinonia, Manchester
Printed in Great Britain
by Biddles Ltd, King's Lynn

Contents

List of plates

Photographs courtesy of the BFI Stills Collection (London). By permission from *Nouvelles Editions de Films* (Paris). If any proper acknowledgement has not been made, copyright-holders are invited to contact the publisher.

Series editors' foreword

To an anglophone audience, the combination of the words 'French' and 'cinema' evokes a particular kind of film: elegant and wordy, sexy but serious – an image as dependent on national stereotypes as is that of the crudely commercial Hollywood blockbuster, which is not to say that either image is without foundation. Over the past two decades, this generalised sense of a significant relationship between French identity and film has been explored in scholarly books and articles, and has entered the curriculum at university level and, in Britain, at A level. The study of film as an art-form and (to a lesser extent) as industry, has become a popular and widespread element of French Studies, and French cinema has acquired an important place within Film Studies. Meanwhile, the growth in multi-screen and 'art-house' cinemas, together with the development of the video industry, has led to the greater availability of foreign-language films to an English-speaking audience. Responding to these developments, this series is designed for students and teachers seeking information and accessible but rigorous critical study of French cinema, and for the enthusiastic filmgoer who wants to know more.

The adoption of a director-based approach raises questions about *auteurism*. A series that categorises films not according to period or to genre (for example), but to the person who directed them, runs the risk of espousing a romantic view of film as the product of solitary inspiration. On this model, the critic's role might seem to be that of discovering continuities, revealing a necessarily coherent set of themes and motifs which correspond to the particular genius of the individual. This is not our aim: the *auteur* perspective on film, itself most clearly articulated in France in the early 1950s, will be interrogated in certain volumes of the series, and, throughout, the director will be treated as one highly significant element in a complex process of film production and reception which includes socio-economic and political determinants, the work of a large and highly skilled team of artists and technicians, the mechanisms of production and distribution, and the complex and multiply determined responses of spectators.

The work of some of the directors in the series is already known outside France, that of others is less so – the aim is both to provide informative and original English-language studies of established figures, and to extend the range of French directors known to anglophone students of cinema. We intend the series to contribute to the promotion of the informal and formal study of French films, and to the pleasure of those who watch them.

DIANA HOLMES
ROBERT INGRAM

Acknowledgements

I would like to thank the following: series editors Diana Holmes and Robert Ingram for their support and intellectual guidance; Kate E. Fox at Manchester University Press for her friendly and professional editorial assistance; Marie-Christine Breton of Nouvelles Editions de Films (NEF) for her interest in, and help with, my work; the staff of the British Film Institute, the French Institute, London, and the British Library; and Annabel Hobley, of the BBC, for kindly locating the documentary: *Arena: My Dinner with Louis* (1984). University College Chichester were most considerate in financing some of the research expenses associated with the preparation of this study.

The writing of this book was also strengthened by many other friends and colleagues. Pilar Munoz, Christopher Flood and Richard Golsan encouraged me from the outset and later provided some helpful documentation. In addition, Stéfan Moriamé kindly contributed with assistance with translation and moral support. Special thanks goes to Benjamin Noys and Barbara Rassi. Benjamin Noys has been an invaluable intellectual companion in my work. One way or another many of his ideas have found their way into this book. Barbara Rassi has frequently helped deepen my thinking on Malle. Her thoughtful perspective on his films was welcome throughout. Indeed, her contribution goes far beyond the world of Louis Malle. Faults will no doubt remain; they are the responsibility of the author. The book is for Alfreda, Joy, Egon and Barbara.

HUGO FREY
March 2004

1

In the eye of the storm

In this book I will introduce readers to the cinema of Louis Malle (1932–95). Malle needs little further preliminary discussion here. His is a body of work that most film critics around the world recognise as being one of the most productive in post-war international cinema, including as it does triumphs such as *Ascenseur pour l'échafaud* (1957); *Le Feu follet* (1963); *Lacombe Lucien* (1974); *Atlantic City USA* (1980) and *Au revoir les enfants* (1987) (Williams 1992: 343; French 1996: 36; LaSalle 1995: 3; Audé 1996: 54–6). As Derek Malcolm underlined shortly after Malle's untimely death: 'his legacy now seems extraordinarily rich – more than thirty films, a half a dozen of them classics' (1995: 32). Moreover, Malle is one of the few directors to have moved effortlessly from French independent production to an extended period of work in the United States. A professional triumph that is only matched by his versatile exchanges from fiction to documentary film, and vice versa. Malle's important contributions to that less glamorous field of media production contain, among others, the extensive television mini-series devoted to contemporary India, *L'Inde fantôme* (1968), as well as documentary feature films devoted to France and the United States.

Malle's work attracted intense public controversy, with a new Malle film being just as likely to find itself debated on the front page of *Le Monde* or *Libération* as reviewed in the film section of those newspapers. Viewed in historical retrospect, Malle is a director who was consistently in the eye of the storm. In this opening chapter I highlight four turbulent periods that mark out the career: the New Wave; May '68; the 1970s; and finally Malle's experience of film-making in the USA and his return to work on selected projects in France (1978–95). The historical and cultural analysis I pursue will position Malle in relation to the dominant social and cultural forces of his times in the two countries in which he worked. It also allows me to draw out several of the important areas of further investigation that form the subjects of subsequent chapters. Already in the course of this overview, tensions, paradoxes and contradictions are in evidence in Malle's career. The words 'Louis Malle' and 'ambiguity' will be frequently brought together in the pages of this book. Ambiguity is a key feature of Mallean cinema that one can first identify, at the very beginning of his career, in his unique relationship with the New Wave.

The New Wave: 'within and without'

Louis Malle's early career falls on the borderline between the innovations of the New Wave and a less precisely defined renewal of postwar French cinema. Work such as his debut feature *Ascenseur pour l'échafaud* anticipated the films of Claude Chabrol, François Truffaut, Jean-Luc Godard and others. Conversely, Malle did not always correspond to the popular aesthetic codes of the mature New Wave. By the beginning of the 1960s, Malle was increasingly antagonistic towards his contemporaries, taking up hostile public positions against the very idea of the New Wave, long before that stance itself became a fashionable pose. In hindsight, each of the discrepancies that exist between Malle and his New Wave contemporaries are exemplary of a director who is frequently difficult to classify. It is for this reason unproductive to try to resolve Malle's ambiguous relationship with his peers. Instead, it is more profitable to dissect how his work simultaneously falls 'within and without' of the New Wave. For it is here, in this paradoxical space, that Louis Malle's engagement with cinema flourished.

In the autumn of 1957 the journalist Françoise Giroud used the phrase *nouvelle vague*, or New Wave, to describe the emergence of a younger generation of professionals in French society. After the term's appearance in the original article for *L'Express* magazine, it soon became a catch-all label to define those young film-makers who were offering their debut features. Within the space of just a few months Claude Chabrol released *Le Beau Serge* (1958) François Truffaut made *Les 400 Coups* (1959) and Jean-Luc Godard presented *A Bout de souffle* (1960). Two years earlier, at the age of just 24, Louis Malle had directed *Ascenseur pour l'échafaud* (1957). The thriller was an instant success and Malle's work was garlanded with the prestigious Prix Louis Delluc. Malle was the youngest post-war recipient of the prize since Marcel Carné. On the occasion of that triumph it had seemed that Malle was the only young hope for French cinema. However, as we know with the benefit of hindsight, by 1959 this privileged status had quickly evaporated, with several other new young directors making commercially successful films (Malle and French 1993: 30–31). Malle's relationship with the birth of the New Wave began with an accident of timing. *Ascenseur pour l'échafaud* was made too soon to be an 'official' New Wave production; but, as I will explain, it was also too close to that phenomenon to be viewed without reference to it.

Comparing Malle's *Ascenseur pour l'échafaud* with Jean-Luc Godard's now iconic *A Bout de souffle* (1960) shows just how central Malle was to the nascent movement in film. Similarities abound between Malle's film and Godard's work. In both cases the directors make significant reference to the American *film noir* tradition, repositioned to the mean streets of contemporary Paris. Their films are high-paced thrillers that focus on comparable strong male anti-heroes. There is a mutual fascination with criminality and youthful rebellion. Furthermore, the central male protagonists from each work are shaped by the wars of decolonisation that France was fighting in Indochina and Algeria (Nicholls 1996: 271–82; Stora 1991: 40). The sense of *ennui* that marked contemporary life during the 1950s, and that was fashionably promoted in Left Bank café philosophy, is another thematic similarity. A common cynicism further draws Godard and Malle's work together. An ironic, fatalistic, tone is a key element in Malle's narrative of coincidences and mistimings. And, as Robin Buss observed, there is a dark amoral realism about the film: 'We are not expected to draw any moral lessons ... but to surrender to its depiction of the new France, of motor ways, glass-fronted buildings, motels and sharp suits, still shackled with antiquated lifts and their dozy attendants. What is wrong with the working-class killer is not that he kills but that he is so incompetent about it' (Buss 1994: 52). Malle's film shares the same mood as Godard's break-through picture. His first success anticipated comparable achievements from his peers.

Technical parallels also link Malle to Godard and the New Wave. For example, Michel Marie underlines the fact that more than any other film from the 1950s *Ascenseur pour l'échafaud* foreshadowed the later fashion for off-studio film-making. This was to soon become a defining characteristic of the new cinema (Marie 1997: 74). Malle's now famous extended tracking shots of Jeanne Moreau walking through the streets of Paris searching for her lover are especially innovative. In fact, they are most obviously comparable to Godard's photography of Jean Seberg in *A Bout de souffle*. Malle's deployment of an improvised Miles Davis jazz soundtrack was a further innovation. Here, again, Malle provided a radical new device that others of his generation would quickly take up. Davis' work on *Ascenseur pour l'échafaud* was without precedent and is credited, along with Roger Vadim's *Et Dieu créa la femme* (1956), with having launched the wider fashion for modern jazz in European cinema (Mouëllic 2000: 84–5). In retrospect, Godard's editing and general pace makes his work more daring and experimental than Malle's film. But the young Malle was also offering innovation and originality to an industry that was entering a period of radical modernisation.

Ascenseur pour l'échafaud carved out radical New Wave territory before the movement had been formally identified. Malle's second feature, *Les Amants* (1958), underlined his position as an emblematic director of the post-war generation. Released at the height of popular and critical discussion of the new cinema and the failure of the older French *cinéastes*, *Les Amants* falls squarely inside the New Wave. The amoral plot that frames the film was ultra modern. Here, Jeanne Tournier (Moreau) abandons her husband, daughter and long-term lover for a third man. He is a casual acquaintance she has met by accident on her return to the family mansion. The following evening, they wander through her gardens and finally make love in her bedroom. In filming what was to prove a revolutionary sequence Malle is accredited with being responsible for providing the first filmic representation of a female orgasm. By today's standards, the portrayal that is found in *Les Amants* is tame. However, in 1958, the same reels of film provoked censorship boards around the world and in so doing brought further fame to Malle. Minister of Culture, André Malraux, attempted to impose restrictions on the film in France, but these were successfully resisted (Gray 1994: 40). However, *Les Amants* was ultimately forbidden for cinema-goers under the age of 16 (Douin 1998: 27). In the United States, the controversy that greeted *Les Amants* meant that Malle was now also a prominent figure on that side of the Atlantic. In fact, *Les Amants* generated one of the most famous trials in the history of American censorship and obscenity law. In 1962, in Cleveland, Ohio, a cinema owner was arrested for showing the film. This case subsequently went to the Supreme Court where two definitive statements on pornography were made in the judgment. Judge Brenner asserted that a film could only be censored for obscenity if it was of absolutely no social importance, which he did not consider to be true of *Les Amants*. Judge Potter Stewart captured the dilemma with the now much quoted phrase: 'I do not know how to define pornography, but I will recognise it when I see it, and the film in question is not pornography' (cited in Douin 1998: 27).

Malle's willingness to handle radical material placed him at the forefront of the crystallising New Wave movement. In the polarised atmosphere of the censorship debate that *Les Amants* initiated many other young directors spoke out in support of Malle's work. For example, François Truffaut memorably called *Les Amants* the 'first night of love in the cinema' and the *Cahiers du cinéma* published an issue devoted to the film, reproducing extracts from its script (Doniol-Valcroze 1958: 43–5). Eric Rohmer was similarly enthusiastic when writing on the merits of *Les Amants* for the review *Arts*. Attacking the favourite *bête noire* of the younger directors, Claude Autant-Lara, Rohmer proclaimed:

> *Les Amants* est un film très important. Il marque, non l'entrée en lice, mais la prise de pouvoir d'une nouvelle génération dans un cinéma français qui semblait, depuis la guerre, le champ clos des plus de quarante, puis de cinquante ans. A Venise, public et jury ne se sont pas trompés. Ils ont preféré la jeunesse de Louis Malle à la maturité d'Autant-Lara. (Rohmer 1958 cited in Douchet 1998: 110).[1]

For Rohmer the triumph of Malle's film marked a victory for all the younger directors. Intentionally or otherwise, Malle was becoming

1 '*Les Amants* is a very important film. It does not mark the first attack of the new generation of directors, but instead their takeover of power in a French cinema that since the war had been a closed shop for the under forties, then the under fifties. At Venice the public and the Jury were not mistaken. They preferred the youth of Louis Malle to the maturity of Autant-Lara'.

part of the new cinema, his work being recuperated by one side of the debate to be used against the other. The impression that Malle was 'one of us', a fully-fledged New Wave man, was accentuated by his choice of material for his third and fourth pictures. In *Zazie dans le métro* (1960) and *Vie privée* (1961) Malle tackled two of the era's most popular cultural attractions. His third picture was an adaptation of Raymond Queneau's best-selling comic novel of the same title. Shot in colour, *Zazie* enhanced Malle's reputation as an ambitious and experimental director. It was less successful at the box-office, failing to gain an audience outside of Paris. *Vie privée* was similarly contemporary in its subject matter. Now, Malle intersected with another New Wave obsession: Brigitte Bardot. *Vie privée* is the quasi-biographical, quasi-fictional, portrayal of her rise to stardom. Starring the eponymous actress, alongside Marcello Mastroianni, Malle's film tried to suggest that behind the public myth there was a frightened and timid girl unable to find her place in the world.

Malle selected highly topical material to film in the late 1950s. Combined with *Ascenseur* and *Les Amants*, this propensity explains why for many critics he is unproblematically a New Wave director (Williams 1992; Wiegand 2001). For the reasons that I have drawn out, the assessment is perfectly accurate. However, Malle was also a far more puzzling figure. The young Malle's place in film history is more problematic and far harder to resolve than one might assume from the material I have raised up to now. Important biographical, social and professional details distinguish Malle from his New Wave contemporaries.

Malle's life and work is shaped by a novel career trajectory, significantly distinctive from a Chabrol, a Truffaut or a Rohmer. On 30 October 1932, Françoise Malle (née Béghin) gave birth to her son Louis. Malle was born into a privileged social environment. Françoise Béghin was a member of the famous Béghin sugar production dynasty and so Louis Malle was heir to a large personal fortune. Louis Malle was the son of a *grand patron*, part of a powerful industrial family whose economic position in the north of France was probably second to none. It was in this upper bourgeois milieu that Malle was first introduced to film. As a child he and his brothers played with their father's 8mm home camera (Malle 1978: 14). More importantly, financial security shaped Malle's early career. Following an enrolment to study history at the Sciences Po' institute, Paris, Malle confidently joined the national film academy, the *Institut des Hautes Etudes Cinématographiques* (IDHEC). While still a student at IDHEC, Malle's first professional codirection and coproduction credits are frankly remarkable. Aside from a student film, *Crazéologie*, Malle was invited to work with the oceanographic director Jacques Yves Cousteau (Billard 2003: 115–16; 119). In 1954–5 Cousteau and Malle filmed the documentary *Le Monde du Silence*. That now dated undersea world extravaganza won Malle a codirector's share of a Palme d'Or award at the Cannes Film Festival (1956) and a Best Documentary Film Oscar at the Academy Awards (1957).

After *Le Monde du silence* Malle continued his upwardly mobile journey with a brief period as assistant director to Robert Bresson on *Un condamné à mort s'est échappé* (1956). Perhaps more importantly for longer term security, the Malle family created their own independent production company, the Nouvelles Editions de Films (NEF) that served Malle's career from that point onwards, including financing Bresson's film (Billard 2003: 152). Malle gained greater financial independence than most other film-makers, and at a far earlier stage of his career. Even before the full formation of NEF, while still an IDHEC student, he had assisted in the production of *Le Monde du silence*. For a Truffaut, a Chabrol or a Rohmer, writing film criticism and the 'student club' atmosphere of the *Cahiers du cinéma* review had been the shared point of professional departure. Malle was never part of that club and one quickly understands why for that reason alone several film historians overlook his contribution to the New Wave (Monaco 1978; Reader 1979: 138; Toubiana 1998).

Malle was also reluctant to be perceived as being part of a group phenomenon in film and showed little interest in debating theory. Any initial attraction Malle had for the idea of a new movement in contemporary cinema was quickly exchanged for a more ironic, stand-offish, attitude. Malle came to this conclusion at the height of the popularity of discussing the 'young cinema' when attending the Cannes festival in 1959. After following discussions on the new cinema, he quickly rejected the debate (Frodon 1995: 22–3). Later that summer, when Malle did participate in a published roundtable on the future of the cinema, he was sceptical about the idea of there having even been an artistic revolution or new school of thought. He asserted that: 'Une nouvelle école se caractérise par le bouleversement des règles esthétiques. Or, jusqu'ici *Hiroshima mon amour* est le seul film

ou la matière du cinéma ait été changé' (Malle 1959: 9).² And, in the
same interview with *Le Monde*, he continued: 'Il serait absurde de
classer les nouveaux auteurs. Ils viennent de partout, vont dans les
directions différentes' (Malle 1959: 9).³ Provocatively, Malle claimed
that it had in fact been the willingness of audiences to watch the work
of the young directors that distinguished the period. Making a quick
political point on the nature of contemporary France, he jibed:

> En France les superproductions italiennes tournées en Yugoslavie par
> des acteurs américains n'intéressaient plus personne. Notre pays – si
> en retard sur tous les points essentiels – me paraît sur ce plan-là tout a
> fait d'avant-garde. Les spectateurs se conduisent bien. Le public
> français a fait le succès de Fellini, de Bergman. (Malle 1959: 9)⁴

The commentaries that Malle offered *Le Monde* suggest that the
collegiate nature of the young generation of *cinéastes* has been over-
estimated by some enthusiastic film scholars in search of clearly
defined schools of thought and shared doctrinal outlooks. Looking
back on the late 1950s, actress Jeanne Moreau has more wisely
underlined the deeply competitive and ambitious qualities of the
directors that she was to work with (Malle and Truffaut). Rather than
seeking collective artistic fame, Moreau emphasises Malle's strong
ambitions to be *the* leading director of his day (Moreau cited in de
Baecque and Toubiana 1996: 203). Perhaps burning ambition
mitigated against any genuine form of artistic collaboration with
potential rivals. Thus, Malle occupied the position of a strategically
'self-exiled' outsider from the *Cahiers du cinéma* clique. Anxious to
preserve his independence from his fellow directors, he did not want
to see his already highly regarded work collapsed into an amorphous
group project. Having already found fame with *Le Monde du silence*
and *Ascenseur pour l'échafaud*, as well as obtained a sound financial

2 'A new school characterises itself by an upheaval of aesthetic rules. So, until now
  Hiroshima mon amour is the only film in which the matter of cinema has been
  changed.'

3 'It would be absurd to class together the new *auteurs*. They come from all over,
  and are going in different directions'.

4 'In France, Italian super-productions, filmed in Yugoslavia with American
  actors, no longer interest anyone. Our country, so backwards on the essential
  questions – seems to me to be in this area absolutely at the forefront. The
  audiences know how to behave. The French public made the success of Fellini,
  of Bergman.'

base for future production, collaboration with rivals would have served little purpose.

Nonetheless Malle developed an important informal and undefined coterie of colleagues. Malle was close to Alain Cavalier, his assistant director on *Ascenseur pour l'échafaud*, and a fellow IDHEC student. Cavalier continued working in film and his career was assisted by Malle. In 1962, Malle's production company, Nouvelles Editions de Films supported Cavalier's first picture, *Le Combat dans l'île*. Jean-Paul Rappeneau is a further artist with connections to Malle's cinema of the 1950s. Best known as the director of the Gérard Depardieu vehicle, *Cyrano de Bergerac* (1991), Rappeneau collaborated with Malle on the script of *Zazie dans le métro* (1960). Subsequently, Rappeneau launched his directorial career, also in collaboration with Cavalier, with the war-time comedy *La Vie d'un Château* (1966). On the release of that film Malle offered his two former colleagues a warm review in *L'Avant-Scène du cinéma* (1966: 6). On the international stage, German Volker Schlöndorff worked with Malle on *Zazie dans le métro*. Another pupil from the IDHEC stable, Schlöndorff's first direction credit was an adaptation of Robert Musil's novel *Der Junge Törless* (*The Young Törless*) (1961). Like Cavalier's *Le Combat dans l'île*, that film was produced by Malle's NEF company. By the end of the 1960s Malle's younger brother, Vincent, assisted Schlöndorff on *Michael Kohlhaas – Der Rebell* (1969).

The collaborations from the late 1950s indicate Malle's willingness to work with selected colleagues and to create personal and professional friendships within the industry. Malle was never an official member of the *Cahiers du cinéma* axis of the New Wave. However, he was an increasingly influential figure for a different but arguably just as important sub-group of first-time directors – directors whose work has been somewhat overshadowed by the predominance of the *Cahiers du cinéma* clique.

Malle's early films present further problems of classification. The aesthetic tone evidenced in his work does not fall comfortably into the mainstream of New Wave practice. Richard Neupert explains the problem with *Zazie dans le métro*: 'This film ... was brightly coloured, silly ... and did not seem to fit what one expected from Malle, much less the New Wave' (2002: 134). The less well-known *Vie privée* is even more distant from New Wave aesthetics. Overlooked by Neupert, it is also shot in colour and, more importantly I think, shot in a formal dramatic style that comes closer to the mainstream classical tradition than to the look of the New Wave hinted at in *Ascenseur pour l'échafaud*. Furthermore, Malle's propensity to tackle superficially different subjects in his films led critics to find his oeuvre difficult to come to terms with. No two films could be more different from each other than *Le Feu follet* (1963) and *Viva Maria* (1965). The former is a dark tragedy, focusing on the last days of a suicide. The latter is a quick-paced historical adventure film, a musical-comedy-western starring Brigitte Bardot and Jeanne Moreau as the 'two Marias', show-girl artists and gun-toting revolutionaries on the wild frontier. Such dramatic disparities in material were rare for a New Wave director. They imply that Malle had completely abandoned the desire to establish his credentials as an *auteur* by repeatedly exploring comparable themes across a set of films. In fact, as I will explain in the next chapter of this book, when discussing Mallean aesthetics in greater detail, it would be wrong to overemphasise the surface differences that exist between Malle's films. There I explain that although Mallean film-making might look like an exercise in eclecticism, over the years a set of consistent aesthetic patterns shine through. During the original sound and fury of the New Wave there was little time for critical reflection and, on the surface at least, Malle looked like an increasingly idiosyncratic director.

Malle *was* a key figure of the New Wave generation but only problematically so. Despite his wary attitude to the idea of a cinematic movement, many of his films were frequently popularly associated with the New Wave in the press and in the minds of the cinema-going public. *Ascenseur pour l'échafaud* and *Les Amants* remain central works of the era. It was also on the back of the more general spirit of the New Wave assault on an older generation of directors that Malle's career first developed. However, the context in which Malle made his first features is complex. His career emerged from a unique position of financial security. Similarly, it is distinctive from the main current of New Wave directors (Truffaut, Chabrol, Godard or Rohmer) because of the exceptionally early international triumph achieved with *Le Monde du silence*. Few directors begin their careers with an internationally famous documentary, let alone an oceanographic one. Moreover, Malle expressed major reservations about the New Wave and was more at home in the company of fellow IDHEC student, Alain Cavalier, than debating *auteur* theory in the pages of *Cahiers du cinéma*.

Malle was 'within and without' of the New Wave and it would be wrong to overemphasise either side of the equation in the search for tidy but inaccurate commentary. Perhaps the most valuable lesson of contextualising Malle's first films is that one discovers a director who offers few easy answers. His ambiguous relationship with his contemporaries is just the first of numerous similar difficult encounters discussed in the course of this book. Nonetheless, whether Malle appreciated the fact or not, much of the rest of his career was founded in the rebirth that French cinema experienced in the late 1950s.

May '68

Within a decade of Malle's first series of triumphs, the director was to experience something akin to a nervous breakdown (Malle and French 1993: 64). Reflecting on the shooting of the historical drama *Le Voleur* (1967), Malle has spoken of his growing dissatisfaction with film-making and the impact an increasingly turbulent private life was having on his work. In retrospect, it seemed to Malle that by 1967 he had come to a private and professional crisis. On the one hand, marriage and divorce had taken their toll. Likewise, the initial optimism of the New Wave had quickly dissipated and became lost in further internecine debate and enmity. In short, by the mid-1960s, independent film-making had entered a different, more difficult phase. With General de Gaulle's return to the Presidency of the Republic (1958) and the end of the war in Algeria (1962), the mid-1960s were a more politically stable but culturally conservative era.

When working on the historical drama *Le Voleur* (1967), Malle started to question himself. Years later when talking to Philip French, he revealed a conversation with his cameraman, Henri Decae:

I said to Henri, 'Do you remember, Henri, I don't know how many years back, something like eight years, in 1958, on the same sound stage, pretty much at the same place, we were putting down rails for a tracking shot for *Les Amants*? And he said 'God you're right, it was this stage, yes.' I said, 'You see, all these years and we've come back to where we started.' It was something to think about. It scared me ... I was beginning to repeat myself. And what did my future hold? Becoming one of the major French directors, making films one after

the other. I decided I had to shake everything up, question everything.
(Malle and French 1993: 65–6)

Malle was far from the only figure in France questioning his social
and professional identity at the end of the 1960s. This personal and
professional drift anticipated a wider generational malaise that
culminated in the *événements* of May '68. However, before considering
that event, and Malle's participation in it, one must underline that
Malle's artistic crisis occurred earlier than May '68 and was combined
with a further dynamic factor, the director's first visit to India.

No less unsettled after the completion of another commercial film,
William Wilson in the portmanteau film, *Histoires Extraordinaires*
(1967 Malle directed this sequence alongside work from Vadim and
Fellini), Malle agreed to represent France on a cultural tour to show
off the New Wave to Indian cinephiles. The shock of India, combined
with Malle's pre-existing sense of personal and professional crisis,
stimulated a passionate return to film-making in the field of
documentary. Working with a small crew, Malle began shooting
scenes of the life that was all around him. India offered a completely
different world to any of Malle's previous experiences and proved a
cathartic release from the tensions that had built up at home. The
practical result of India was many hours of documentary footage that
was subsequently edited into two film projects: the cinema-released –
Calcutta (1968) and the television series, *L'Inde fantôme* (1968).

India, and a return to documentary film-making years after *Le
Monde du silence*, provided Malle with a new environment which
broke the sense of stagnation that he had experienced when filming
Le Voleur. Extra-filmic events – in French society and politics – provided
another dramatic influence that was to impact on his life and work.
Returning to France to edit his material from India, Malle first participated in the controversy that was raging around the directorship of
the National Cinémathèque. Henri Langlois, its director, had been
removed by the Gaullist Minister of Culture, André Malraux, and a
battle raged over his reinstatement. Alongside many of his former
New Wave rivals, Malle signed petitions in support of the reinstatement of Langlois and participated in the patronage committee of the
campaign for reinstatement of the director. As with his turn to the
documentary, this radicalisation was a relatively new departure that
suggested another less mainstream side to the director. Malle's
participation in this cause was markedly different from his previous

refusal in the early 1960s to sign petitions in opposition to the French war in Algeria (see Truffaut 1989: 152; Billard 2003: 219–20). After the Langlois affair another opportunity presented itself for Malle to explore his new more radical persona. As a member of the jury at the Cannes Film Festival (May 1968), Malle assisted in suspending the event in sympathy with the wider social revolt that was developing on a daily basis in Paris. On the 18 May 1968, Malle, alongside Truffaut, Godard, Claude Berri, Claude Lelouch, Gabriel Albicocco and a reluctant Roman Polanski called for a suspension of the festival. Soon after the suspension, Malle returned to Paris where he joined the meetings of the 'Estates General of cinema'. Inspired by the atmosphere of revolution Malle was a keen participant at the meetings of the cinema group. On 26 May 1968, he was a co-signatory of a paper to the assembly of the Estates General of Cinema. In it he offered a vision of film-making that was very different from his roots in the bourgeoisie or his career as a film producer. His detailed motion to the floor argued for the creation of a 'secteur public' in film and television (see Frodon 1995: 236; Billard 2003: 292–8; published verbatim in *Cahiers du cinéma* June 1968; as well as anecdotal discussion in Carrière 2003: 54–5; 62).

Malle's actions during the Cannes Festival and in the Estates General show that he had almost completely abandoned his reputation as the popular director of films like the star-vehicle, Moreau–Bardot comedy, *Viva Maria* (1965). Now, in the light of personal crisis, India and May '68, Malle planned a codirection with Pierre Kast of a cinematic exploration of a fantasy South American utopian community (Malle and French 1993: 81). Although the Kast collaboration was never realised other projects that chimed strongly with the mood of the May '68 counter-culture were completed. The documentaries on India were edited and distributed. They contain loosely, abstractly argued political commentaries that evidence the new radical climate, rejecting western capitalist industrialisation and glorifying religious mysticism. Typical too of the popular political atmosphere was a further documentary on daily life in a Citroën car factory, *Humain, trop humain* (1974), as well as a documentary snapshot of Parisian street life, *Place de la République* (1974).

The late 1960s witnessed the emergence of a new Louis Malle that was different from the ambitious young man of the 1950s. A reluctance for political engagement was exchanged for a more complicated set of social and cultural values that chimed with the national political Zeitgeist. Having profited from, but also rejected the New Wave, and refused to directly protest against the war in Algeria, Malle now joined the new post-May '68 film union, La Société des Réalisateurs du Film (SRF). Although the SRF was more of a professional organisation than a 'gauchiste' group, its programme called for the protection of a director's moral rights of authorship and was strongly opposed to state censorship (Frodon 1995: 238). Perhaps it was this libertarian edge that led Malle in 1970 to also campaign alongside Jean-Paul Sartre, Simone de Beauvoir and others, to allow the continued publication of the ultra-left newspaper, *La Cause du peuple* (see Drake 2002: 141). Two years later Malle was approached by director Joseph Losey to be part of another independent directors' guild. Malle's reply to the proposal remains unknown (Caute 1994: 319). Less obviously radicalised by the wider social climate than Jean-Luc Godard, Malle is nevertheless one of the few film-makers who found themselves shaped by the politics of May '68 and whose career dramatically intersected with it (Jeancolas 1995: 83).

In the midst of these significant changes, I think it is important to identify an important element of consistency between the late 1950s and the late 1960s. Malle's new films and other unfinished projects, including the India documentaries, were just as evocative of their times as *Ascenseur pour l'échafaud* had been of France *circa* 1957. In some ways here was a typical 'soixante-huitard' ('May Sixty-Eighter') at work: a self-reflexive documentary film-maker first exploring Indian mysticism and next the drudgery of life on the Citroën factory assembly line. Symbolically speaking, Malle replaced the 'New Wave look', the dinner jackets, Jaguar motorcar and Martinis of the 1950s with a beard, jeans and T-shirt. However, the new style was just as exemplary of its time and place as the old one had been. Regarding the film-making agenda, major changes of material (from fiction to documentary) and form (from more formal dramatic mode to '*cinéma direct*' documentary) *had* occurred. However, Malle was still finding himself in the midst of key contemporary political and cultural trends. During ten years of cultural, social and political transformation Malle had kept himself in the eye of the storm. As we will see in Chapter 3 of this book the deeper political shift Malle underwent from ambiguous New Wave playboy to 'soixante-huitard' radical went considerably beyond the level of style and form.

Four provocations from the 1970s

Malle's four major films of the 1970s can be read as a synthesis of his earlier work. They represent a fusion of the youthful bravado and confidence of the 1950s combined with the new political questioning adopted in the late 1960s. *Le Souffle au cœur* (1971), *Lacombe Lucien* (1974), *Black Moon* (1975) and *Pretty Baby* (1978) were made in relatively quick succession and each engaged in controversial and divisive themes. Following a path established in *Les Amants*, Malle again systematically pushed film censors, classifying boards and audiences towards new and original ways of imagining the world. Taken together the four films from the 1970s are a sustained challenge to conventional thinking and conservatism.

Le Souffle au cœur offered a wry exploration of the 1950s bourgeois family and the sexual initiation of a teenage boy. Notoriously, the film ends with an incident of incest between the boy and his mother. This transgression goes unpunished and the family seems less dysfunctional than before the act. Three years later, in the historical drama *Lacombe Lucien* Malle focused on a young peasant collaborator and provoked much criticism from defenders of the honour of the French resistance. *Black Moon* and *Pretty Baby*, although very different films, confirmed Malle's new reputation as a radical controversialist. In *Black Moon* Malle depicts a fantasy dream world that has been torn apart by a violent war of the sexes. It concludes with the powerful, disturbing image of a young woman (15-year-old British actress Cathryn Harrison) offering her naked breast to the suckling mouth of a magical unicorn. *Pretty Baby* represented Malle's final assault on 'good taste' and is one of his most disturbing films. Shot on location in the United States, and produced by Paramount, it was Malle's first English-language work. Its plot focuses on a child's experience of growing up in a turn-of-the-century New Orleans brothel and her subsequent relationship with the photographer E. J. Bellocq.

In all four pictures much is left to the viewer's imagination. But, as most good directors know, this strategy is a far more disturbing choice than the 'showing all' alternative. *Le Souffle au cœur* is filmed as social comedy, while *Lacombe Lucien* does not indulge in extreme violence. Given that *Pretty Baby* starred the 11-year-old child actress Brooke Shields, Malle did not have much room to manoeuvre within US legal requirements. The film does, however, include brief scenes of nudity in a quasi-sexual context. In Canada it was banned and to my knowledge was never released there. During the controversy that followed, Malle defended himself with explanations such as: 'it must be the only film shot solely in a brothel where there is not one scene showing the next act [i.e sexual intercourse]' (Malle cited in Vine 1979: 1). Elsewhere he pointed out that the Canadians had been unable to identify any scenes to cut. His work was subtle and did not include any especially graphic visual material and hence the dilemma for the censors.

Why did Malle take up these interlinking topics? Why then? Perhaps the first question is the easier to respond to. Regarding motivation, Malle has suggested that they each responded to his experiences of childhood and his psychological working through of that period. *Le Souffle au cœur* is a good illustrative example. Malle has explained that this film emerged from his own sense of post-May '68 crisis and more specifically from the return of his repressed memories of his youth. Just like the boy in the film Malle had been troubled by a heart murmur and had for a period of time in the late 1940s been educated at home so as to assist his convalescence. At the age of 13 he had spent some time in a health spa and had indeed shared a bedroom with his mother (Malle and French 1993: 83). If one follows Malle's account of the origins of the film, it was the repressed memory of this period and indirectly also that of his childhood experiences living through the Nazi occupation of France that led to this quasi-autobiographical fiction.

Malle's explanation for returning to fiction in 1971 is repeated when exploring his motivations for the other three films from the 1970s. Generally speaking, his retrospective view of the films from this period is that they were reflections of his inner life, or, far more generally speaking, responses to his intellectual and artistic interests. For example, Georges Bataille's novel *Ma mère* (1935) is cited by Malle as the intertextual source that also stimulated *Le Souffle au cœur*. Similarly, Lewis Carroll's *Alice in Wonderland* (1865) is a reference point for both *Black Moon* and, to a lesser extent, *Pretty Baby*. Other motivations for *Pretty Baby* were Malle's love of jazz and an interest in the Storyville district of New Orleans, inspired by Al Rose's academic study (1974). It also represented an opportunity to work in the United States, a plan Malle had frequently considered since the international notoriety he had gained there during the *Les Amants* controversy.

Malle's statements at the times of the initial release of these films also suggests an important post-'68 cultural–political dynamic, an explanation that is glossed over in Malle's later interviews with Philip French. Thus, at time of release, Malle explained that *Le Souffle au cœur* was not just an exercise in autobiography, or a reworking of the Georges Bataille source text, but also a more calculated attack on the idea of middle-class sexual taboos. In counterpoint to traditional Catholic notions of the family and sexual self-control, Malle used his film to argue for a libertarian position that was loosely influenced by Wilhelm Reich's writings on childhood and sexual freedom (Malle 1971: 1). Part of the point of the film, as Malle voiced it in 1971 was to show that alternative structures of sexuality were possible. While not literally advocating incest, Malle implied that alternative models of sexuality were not necessarily psychologically damaging, let alone sinful in an orthodox Christian sense. Therefore, according to Malle the film was an ironic denunciation of bourgeois morality (Malle 1971: 2). Furthermore, Malle marshalled some of the slogans of May '68 to justify his material. He explained that his film was confronting the contemporary world and its taboos: 'Notre société est dans une impasse totale mais s'il y a une chose que j'ai retenu de mai 68, c'est: l'imagination au pouvoir' (Malle 1971: 2).[5]

It is plausible to see each film from the 1970s quartet as weapons in a wider socio-sexual assault on the French and western taboos of incest, fascism and the occupation, or the regulation of childhood sexuality within bourgeois power structures. In truth, this was a vague, undefined, engagement, that was not conducted on the level of party politics, and that is not easily mapped onto the left–right political spectrum. It is a far more complicated and confused attempt to question fundamental notions of contemporary western society. The programme that Malle pursued was not linked to any straightforward political orthodoxy and Malle never abandoned his rejection of Communism. Instead, it tended to address specific taboos consistently so as to show them in a more complicated and ambiguous light. With hindsight it is therefore far easier to identify the groups or subjects that Malle was attacking (the hypocrisy of middle-class sexual desire and moral rectitude; Gaullist and Communist

5 'Our society is at a total dead-end, an impasse. But if there is one thing that I have held on to from May '68, it's: Power to the Imagination.'

visions of a *France résistante*) but much more difficult to establish a positive agenda. Indeed, this seemingly random, individualistic radicalism is partially confirmed by Malle's only widely recorded traditional political intervention from the period. In the form of a brief essay for *Le Monde* Malle offered his support to the first French ecologist candidate to the Presidency, the long-since forgotten René Dumont (Malle 1974b; Billard 2003: 359). However, Malle used the opportunity to attack the other candidates and said relatively little about the virtues of Dumont's own policies.

Malle's development into a troubling 1970s *agent provocateur* cannot be divorced from the context of cinema at that time. Despite the originality of Malle's work I think its spirit was deeply marked by the period in which it was made. A brief survey of the trade journal, *Le Film Français* is a helpful way of providing a flavour of the period. A rapid leaf through the pages of film advertisements reveals how closely Malle's films echo popular themes of the day. Most of the films advertised in the early 1970s included a strong mixture of either explicit sexual content or extreme violence. For comparative purposes one should recall that 1971 was the year of the violent western *Soldier Blue* (directed by Ralph Nelson and starring Malle's later wife, Candice Bergen) as well as *The Music Lovers* (directed by Ken Russel) which featured infamous scenes of nudity. Anticipating *Lacombe Lucien*, the Italian director, Bernardo Bertolucci had already offered his exploration of sexuality and fascism in *Il Conformista (The Conformist)* (1970). In 1973, Bertolucci's next release was the notorious *Last Tango in Paris*. Other Italian directors, Luchino Visconti and Liliana Cavani, presented their interpretations of fascism and sado-masochistic titillation in films that were quickly compared to Malle's own study of collaborationism. Outside the high-brow mainstream, the 'erotic' and pornographic film industry, fuelled by the arrival of the Swedish distributor Francis Mischkind's films in France, was also reaching a peak. As a director from that sector of the film industry has colourfully explained in his memoirs: 'Nous voudrions dynamiter le mur d'ordre moral' (Leroi 1999: 42).[6] When presented in a context in which the 'soft-porn' film *Emmanuelle* was the mainstream box-office hit of 1974, *Black Moon* or *Pretty Baby* look less distinctive. On the other hand, one must highlight the fact that Malle's battles with

---

6 'We wanted to blow up the wall of the moral order.'

censors over originally *Les Amants* and, later in 1971, *Le Souffle au cœur* had to an extent paved the way for his contemporaries.[7]

Notwithstanding social mores, artistic merit or intellectual importance, the topics Malle was now handling helped reinvent the director into a prominent and marketable commodity of 1970s cinema. By 1978, world cinema had changed completely in its representation of sexual intercourse and violence and Malle's choice of subject matter in *Pretty Baby* maintained his position in the face of ever more extreme rival productions. In the United States, William Friedkin's *The Exorcist* (1973) had set a new trend for the horror film, Steven Spielberg had offered the blockbuster *Jaws* (1975) and Martin Scorcese had already cast a teenage Jodie Foster in *Taxi Driver* (1976). Each of these films had used children or teenage actors and presented their bodies as the sites of extreme violence, and in the case of *The Exorcist* bourgeois sexual anxiety as well. Back in France, even Malle's brother, Vincent, had produced an erotic comedy, *Les Bijoux de famille* (directed by Malle's regular sound-man, Jean-Claude Laureux, 1974). In comparison, Malle's *Pretty Baby* looks less original or challenging than one might first think. It can be seen as an attempt on Malle's part to position himself dramatically in the new North American market and to ensure a powerful commercial footing there.

By 1978, rather as in the 1950s, Malle was making news, dating his leading actress (Susan Sarandon from *Pretty Baby*) and capturing the attention of his peers and audiences alike. The costumes and scenery might have changed but the basic plot of Malle's life was familiar. Of the four films *Lacombe Lucien* has proven the most enduring and was, in France, at least, the most genuinely divisive and controversial work. This film is analysed at length in Chapter 4, as is *Pretty Baby*. In fact, as I will explain in that chapter, I think scenes from these films remain provocative and harrowing to watch. They continue to fulfil their own loose remit to disturb bourgeois values through their unremitting refusal to offer political or moral judgements.

7 It is easy to forget the state censorship Malle faced when making a film like *Le Souffle au cœur*. For example, Malle did not receive advanced state funding against ticket sales for the project. Similarly, when the television show *Post-Scriptum* invited Malle to discuss incest in the light of his treatment it found itself in political difficulties. Just two weeks after this transmission Michel Polac's chat-show was suspended by the director of French national television (see Hamon and Rotman 1988: 375).

Finally, regarding this period, it is important to underline that Malle's invectives were perfectly timed. His films of the 1970s captured some genuinely radical ground when this was precisely the most chic of cultural options. No doubt Malle helped create the fashion, but he also gained from it. His work was central to the dominant cultural paradigms of the 1950s and the era of May '68. Malle's 1970s provocations share that same sense of cultural timeliness. In this context the status of Malle as a 'rebel director' is considerably nuanced.

America and after ...

Malle's decision to work in the United States on *Pretty Baby* had been initially limited to the making of that film for Paramount. In the director's mind this was a one-off project. However, in the decade that followed *Pretty Baby*, Malle became one of a select group of European directors who settled or worked in the United States. Although Malle's motivations for this were in part driven by his personal circumstances (he was Susan Sarandon's partner, and later husband to Candice Bergen) the move also offered distinct professional opportunities and, rather as India had acted as a force for renewal, the move to America marked a further distinct change in artistic direction.

On first viewing *Atlantic City USA* (1980), *My Dinner with André* (1981), *Crackers* (1983) and *Alamo Bay* (1985) are very different pictures with little immediately in common. However, when read in the context of their production, they are especially notable because they carried forward the tradition of independent cinema of the 1970s into the post-*Jaws* and post-*Star Wars* blockbuster era of 1980s Reaganite Hollywood. Malle produced quirky films which cut right across the mainstream of cinematic fashion. The films from this period are thoughtful explorations of human emotions, told through small stories of ordinary individuals living in contemporary America. Nothing could have been further from the mainstream commercial mood, or in fact from the far more immediately provocative Malle quartet from the 1970s.

Malle's US films succeeded by taking almost the inverse strategy to 1980s popular convention for spectacular entertainment and juvenilia. All Malle's films from this era stand out as serious dramas that do not pander to Hollywood conventions. *Atlantic City USA* is typical. Although a crime story, it is among other things also a quasi-sociological dissection of the city of its title. Very subtly it works as a comment on a number of American myths, the foremost being that of the 'gangster as hero'. Cleverly, Malle cast Burt Lancaster against type as a failing, ageing and incompetent crook. Malle made the American hero, Lancaster, look like a down-at-heel nobody, a small-time hoodlum who had never even fulfilled the promise of the gangster myth on which he had founded his life. Malle's next picture, *My Dinner with André*, took the strategy of inverting spectacular Hollywood cinema to a new extreme. Starring just two middle-age actors, André Gregory and Wallace Shawn, playing themselves, the film is a two-hour portrayal of a conversation over dinner. A dazzling range of intellectual and pseudo-intellectual topics are covered in this mammoth conversation-piece and then, just as suddenly as they arrived at dinner, both men depart, happy that they have met up after all the years. Boldly intellectual in its conception, as well as the conversation itself, the film remains a contemporary classic that perhaps few people even recognise as a Louis Malle picture. On its release the film was a major success, attracting widespread attention in the American media and even provoking house parties that mimicked the themes raised in André and Wally's dinner. Malle had created the perfect 'anti-spectacle' film but in so doing had won perhaps more national recognition than the imitators of Spielberg or Lucas. Malle's inversion of the rules of Hollywood cinema paid off and ironically positioned him as one of the most successful art directors of the era. *Atlantic City USA* or *My Dinner with André* made their mark by establishing their extreme distance from the conventions of mainstream cultural life. They are genuinely original films, although as we will see later in this book they also contained thematic elements that reflect wider Mallean concerns. In particular both these films implicitly expanded on the director's interest in history, more overtly displayed in *Lacombe Lucien*. This is a subject I take up for closer analysis when interpreting the importance of *Atlantic City USA* in Chapter 4. For that film's handling of the historical through exclusive reference to the psychological well-being of its protagonists represents an important movement in Mallean film.

Malle's *Alamo Bay* (1985) was a far stronger piece than *Crackers* (1983) and was also a return to some, now typical Mallean preoccupations. Like the 1970s quartet it is a 'problem film' which posed difficult questions about a controversial political theme. Set in a small fishing community on the Gulf of Mexico the film focuses on an impossible romance between the wife of a 'red-neck' racist Klansman and a Vietnamese immigrant fisherman. Unlike the 1970s pictures that Malle had made the piece has a contemporary setting. However, rather like Malle's later British picture, *Damage* (1992), the film suffers from being overly formulaic. The theme of 'impossible partners' had been taken up earlier in *Ascenseur pour l'échafaud* (adultery), *Les Amants* (double adultery), *Le Souffle au cœur* (mother and son incest); *Lacombe Lucien* (fascist and Jew) and *Pretty Baby* (adult photographer and child prostitute). Nevertheless, Malle's choice of milieu for *Alamo Bay*, post-Vietnam America, and the subject of race and immigration in the south of the US, were more promising. Made just before the 1980s fashion for Vietnam war movies (captured in Oliver Stone's *Platoon* (1987) and Stanley Kubrick's *Full Metal Jacket* (1989)), those few scholars who have discussed *Alamo Bay* underline its genuinely significant contribution to the formation of that important genre (Palmer 1993: 105). Once again, Malle had captured a political–cultural mood that was soon to produce a flourish of films on the nature of that war and its memory.

Malle's time in America included two major documentaries: *God's Country* (1986) and *And the Pursuit of Happiness* (1987). These films remind us of Malle's contributions to this field and his consistent return to it after *L'Inde fantôme*. Both the documentaries play strongly on the fact that Malle is an outsider, a visitor, exploring America. They are therefore not only about the people and communities that he films but also focus on Malle's own relationship with America. As will be discussed in the light of Malle's wider aesthetic decisions (see Chapter 2), they are therefore far closer to the 'visual journalistic essay' format than to a traditional omniscient-narrator documentary. The two films are also striking because of their detailed focus on specific individuals or small communities. *God's Country* is a study 'in miniature' of the agricultural town of Glencoe and its changing economic fortunes between 1979 and 1985. Similarly, *And the Pursuit of Happiness* is structured around a series of interviews with other 'new Americans' all of whom have settled in that country. These films were not commercial projects and are probably not that important in terms of the complete Mallean oeuvre. Nonetheless, they demonstrate

Malle's continued loyalty to a less popular form of film-making, even while working 'in Hollywood'.

Malle's American oeuvre stands out and contrasts favourably with contemporary Europeans who had made similar moves across the Atlantic. Very few Europeans in the 1980s made equally successful migrations and those that did filmed far more mainstream material than Malle. A brief comparison with the Dutch director, Paul Verhoeven, throws an interesting sidelight on the originality of Malle's work. To date Verhoeven has used his Hollywood career in a far more a conventional way than Malle. He has explained his caution regarding working in Hollywood with more than a hint of admiration for Malle's experience. Thus, the Dutch director justified his willingness to film the spectacular science fiction blockbuster, *Robocop* (1987) in the following terms: 'To start straight away with, say, a story about New Orleans, full of racial issues and social comment seemed a bit ambitious to me' (cited in van Scheers 1997: 183). Where Paul Verhoeven was reluctant, Malle was ambitious and did not especially compromise his vision when working in the United States. It is therefore appropriate that young independent American directors have now started to rediscover Malle. Wes Anderson, the director of *Rushmore* (2000) and *The Royal Tannenbaums* (2002) is the notable example (Anderson 2002: 12). Both Anderson's films owe a great deal to the achievements of Malle and rather cleverly draw on his best work. Thus, in his quirky films Anderson looks to the sophistication and comic lightness of *Le Souffle au cœur*, the experimental vibrance of *Zazie dans le métro* and a hint of the pessimistic melancholy found in *Le Feu follet*.

Had Malle ceased making films in 1986 his reputation would have been secure, grounded in his New Wave pictures and later films like *Le Souffle au cœur*, *Lacombe Lucien* and *Atlantic City USA*. However, Malle continued filming and made four more productions before his premature death of lymphonic cancer in 1995. Among pictures such as *Milou en mai* (1989), *Damage* (1992) and *Vanya on 42nd Street* (1994), it is however *Au revoir les enfants* (1987) that continues to be Malle's best-known and most admired work.

In 1986 Malle returned to France to begin working on a film about his childhood experiences of attending a Catholic boarding school during the Nazi occupation. The intellectual and popular response to *Au revoir les enfants* was overwhelmingly supportive. For a short period, the prodigal son who had left Europe to live and work in America was one of his homeland's best-loved cultural icons. Thus, *Au revoir les enfants* was garnered with seven Césars (the French equivalent to Oscars) and was *the* film of 1987. Malle's sensitive handling of an episode from the *années noires* chimed with a wider political climate that had recently been primed to such issues by the trial of the 'Butcher of Lyons', Klaus Barbie (Rousso 1990: 271). In this highly charged period of the collective memory of the Vichy regime, Malle's film inspired educational projects and became a common part of high school discussions on contemporary history (see Braunschweig and Gidel 1989). In contrast to the more iconoclastic *Lacombe Lucien*, Malle now provided a film that broadly speaking showed that some citizens had resisted the Nazi occupation and had tried to limit the Holocaust in France. Here was a tragic episode from the past but one that also contained much human dignity.

From the perspective of a student of the complete Mallean oeuvre the film is important for other reasons too. *Au revoir les enfants* revealed on screen for the first time an aspect of the director's life that had not been overtly expressed in his previous work. As the film concludes Louis Malle's voice is heard. He explains: 'Bonnet, Négus et Dupré sont morts à Auschwitz, le Père Jean au camp de concentration de Mauthausen. Le collège a rouvert ses portes en octobre 1944. Plus de quarante ans ont passé, mais jusqu'à ma mort je me rappellerai chaque seconde de ce matin de janvier' (Malle 1987: 132–3).[8] As Lynn Higgins has argued, with these words a new psychoanalytical interpretative pattern could be thrown across Malle's career (1992). In the light of the events filmed in *Au revoir les enfants*, Higgins justifiably questioned the extent to which Malle's wartime childhood experiences had shaped all his previous films. At the very least, as Roderick Kedward (2000) has perceptively suggested, *Au revoir les enfants* brought into question the meaning of much of Malle's previous oeuvre. He explains the new dynamic: '*Lacombe Lucien* and *Au revoir les enfants* are, in a sense, the wrong way round: we can understand Lucien much better if we imagine *Au revoir les*

8 'Bonnet, Négus, and Dupré died in Auschwitz, Father Jean in the camp at Mauthausen. The school reopened its doors in October 1944. Over forty years have passed, but I will remember every second of that January morning until the day I die.'

enfants as already made' (2000: 231). After *Au revoir les enfants* biographical study and psychoanalytic theory offer different perspectives on Malle's filmography than a strictly chronological study can relate. This is an approach towards Malle that I will expand on in the fifth and final chapter of this book. Here I will debate the Mallean opus in the light of the director's formative experience of the Nazi occupation and the treatment of this legacy in *Au revoir les enfants*.

Conclusion

For much of Louis Malle's career his films have contributed to major cinematic trends or been closely related to the political–cultural context in which they were made. Malle was a successful director and self-promoting producer and this centrality assisted the longevity of his career. His ability to provide films for their times was an unerring quality that Malle possessed in abundance. It was also a strategy supported by the director's NEF production house, his extensive interviews and associated publicity work (too prolific to do justice to here) that gave audiences 'the necessary glasses with which to watch his films'.[9] However, as a foreign film-maker in Hollywood, already at the height of his European career, Malle offered innovative pictures such as *My Dinner with André* that were as successful as when he worked within more dominant cultural paradigms.

I think that Malle's career trajectory can also be profitably interpreted as a long response to his initial success during the New Wave period. Having achieved major cinematic awards and been a key European film-maker by his twenties and thirties, the eclipse of the New Wave left Malle searching for a new professional identity and context in which to position his art. His evolution saw him adopt a more politically radical stance than might ever have been imagined on the basis of his early work. Malle's ability to reinvent himself as a radical was a success and the four films of the 1970s remain a

9 The phrase is borrowed from the Austrian director Georg Tressler (October 2002, 'In Conversation', Riverside Studios, London). Tressler used it to explain why he felt his films had not found a significant international audience. I think it is a useful reminder of the importance of Malle's own many interviews and press activities. Malle was a producer and director who 'gave numerous glasses to his audiences', inviting them to interpret his films in particular ways.

powerful quartet. The move to the United States in the late 1970s offered another opportunity for change and variation.

Malle's relationship with his times is also a subject marked with ambiguity. His career regularly falls close to the heart of dominant cultural trends or political experiences (New Wave; May '68) but also strangely lies outside them. This characteristic is prominently illustrated in the tensions that existed between Mallean cinema and the New Wave. Malle cannot be understood without reference to that movement but equally his life and work stand apart from it. Contradictions also weigh heavily on Malle's radical turn of the late 1960s and 1970s. On the one hand, in films like *Le Souffle au cœur* or *Lacombe Lucien* Malle was a radical force in the cinematic arts. Conversely, one recalls that this non-conformist position was widely shared by many others throughout the Parisian intellectual and cultural community at this time. So, a further ambiguity arises between Malle's preference for provocative thematic ground and the commercial success this territory attracted. Malle succeeded in making provocative and fashionable films, radical but nonetheless mainstream work. Malle was a social insider who was attracted to make 'outsider' films. These partners are uneasy bedfellows and Malle's status as an outsider was often overshadowed by the dominant mainstream cultural mood that he also tapped into. Perceptively, Malle at times rightly feared his work was open to recuperation by the very social groups he confronted in his work (Malle and French 1993: 55–6). The grounds for that anxiety are confirmed by the historical contexts that I have analysed in this chapter. So, Malle was sometimes a non-conforming conformist, but he was also just as much a conforming non-conformist. There is a radical edge to his work but not exclusively.

The above features of the Malle career are but the first set of ambiguities in an oeuvre littered with contradictions. And, if in a career that was long and diverse there is one recurrent leitmotif to be pursued across the thematic chapters that make up this book, it lies here. Throughout this study I will be interpreting, unpicking and decoding the dynamics of a cinema of ambiguity. In Chapter 2 I discuss the shape of Mallean aesthetics and how that paradigm tends to defy simplistic artistic categorisation. In Chapter 3 I will continue to explore some of the tensions that are intrinsic to Malle's position as a 1970s radical in the light of the politics of his films of the 1950s.

Questions of the portrayal of women in Malle's film are also raised here. Chapter 4 is predominantly devoted to Malle's most ambiguous fictional creation, the boy-scout collaborator, *Lacombe Lucien*. The more troubling implications of Malle's rhetorical pose of ambiguity in that film are highlighted by comparison with *Pretty Baby*. Finally, Chapter 5 concludes this book with a focus on the impact of *Au revoir les enfants* and how it might be used to recast our assumptions about Malle's work; to analyse this controversial director in the light of a psychoanalytic reading of his work. Here, it will be essential to analyse how so much of Mallean cinema seems to be explained by the events depicted in that film.

So, the central *parti pris* that I adopt in this study is to unravel the many ambiguities and contradictions that make up Malle's filmography. Readers seeking an entertaining and thoroughly researched biography should turn to Pierre Billard's, *Louis Malle. Le Rebelle solitaire* (2003). Adding to Billard's work, I aim to show just how challenging and complex Malle's cinema continues to be. In short, readers looking for Malle to be an unproblematic hero of the French cinematic arts will be disappointed. Instead, I think that in Malle we have a far more fascinating subject, a director whose films ask difficult questions and offer few reassuring answers. A director who in the course of this book we will see fighting against any simplification of the meaning of his work. Whatever one might think about Malle today, he continues to represent a most enigmatic and multifaceted artist.

References

Anderson, Wes (2002) 'On Louis Malle's *Le Souffle au cœur* (1971)', *Daily Telegraph*, 9 March, Arts Review: 12.

Audé, Françoise (1996) 'Louis Malle, 1932–1995' *Positif* (January): 54–6.

Bataille, Georges (1935) *Ma mère* (Paris: Gallimard).

Billard, Pierre (2003) *Louis Malle: Le Rebelle solitaire* (Paris: Plon).

Braunschweig, Maryvonne and Bernard Gidel (1989) *Les Déportés d'Avon. Enquête autour du film de Louis Malle, Au revoir les enfants* (Paris: La Découverte).

Buss, Robin (1994) *French Film Noir* (London: Marion Boyars).

Carrière, Jean-Claude (2003) *Les Années d'utopie* (Paris: Plon).

Caute, David (1994) *Joseph Losey* (London: Faber & Faber).

de Baecque, Antoine and S. Toubiana (1996) *François Truffaut* (Paris: Gallimard).

de Baecque, Antoine (1998) *La Nouvelle Vague* (Paris: Flammarion).

Doniol-Valcroze, Jacques (1958) 'Le pouvoir de la nuit', *Cahiers du cinéma*, 15.89: 43–5.

Douchet, Jean (1998) *Nouvelle Vague* (Paris: Editions Hazan).

Douin, Jean-Luc (1998) *Dictionnaire de la censure au cinéma* (Paris: PUF).

Drake, David (2002) *Intellectuals and Politics in Post-War France* (Basingstoke: Palgrave).

French, Philip (1996) 'Louis Malle', *Sight and Sound* 16.3: 36.

Frodon, Jean-Michel (1995) *L'Age Moderne du Cinéma Français: De la Nouvelle Vague à nos jours* (Paris: Flammarion).

Gray, Marianne (1994) *La Moreau: A Biography of Jeanne Moreau* (London: Little Brown and Company).

Hamon, Hervé and Patrick Rotman (1988) *Génération*, vol 2: *Les années de poudre* (Paris: Seuil).

Higgins, Lynn (1992) 'If Looks Could Kill: Louis Malle's Portraits of Collaboration', in Richard Golsan (ed.), *Fascism, Aesthetics and Culture* (Hanover: University Press of New England): 198–212.

Jeancolas, Jean-Pierre (1995) *Histoire du cinéma français* (Paris: Nathan).

Kedward, Roderick (2000) '*Lacombe Lucien* and the Anti-Carnival of Collaboration', in Susan Hayward and Ginette Vincendeau (eds), *French Film: Texts and Contexts* (London: Routledge): 227–39.

LaSalle, Mick (1995) 'The Compassionate Observer', *San Francisco Chronicle*, 25 Nov.: C3.

Leroi, Francis (1999) *'70s Les années érotiques* (Paris: La Musardine).

Malcolm, Derek (1995) 'An Eye for the Inner Character', *Guardian* 25 Nov.: 32.

Malle, Louis (1959) 'L'Avenir du cinéma français. Une table ronde imaginaire entre producteurs et réalisateurs', *Le Monde* 11.8: 1, 9.

Malle, Louis (1966) 'Grâce et précision', *L'Avant-Scène* 58 (April 1966): 6.

Malle, Louis (1971) 'Entretien avec Louis Malle', *Journal du Show Business. L'Hebdomadaire International des professionnels du spectacle* 15 May 1971: 1–3.

Malle, Louis (1974a and 1979) *Audio Tape Interviews from the National Film Theatre* London (London: BFI).

Malle, Louis (1974b) 'Pour Dumont', *Le Monde* 4.5: 11.

Malle, Louis (1978) *Louis Malle par Louis Malle* (Paris: Editions de l'Athanor).

Malle, Louis (1987) *Au revoir les enfants* (Paris: Gallimard).

Malle, Louis and Philip French (1993) *Malle on Malle* (London: Faber & Faber).

Marie, Michel (1997) *La Nouvelle Vague. Une école artistique* (Paris: Editions Nathan).

Monaco, James (1976) *The New Wave* (Oxford: Oxford University Press).

Mouëllic, Gilles (2000) *Jazz et cinéma* (Paris: Cahiers du cinéma).

Neupert, Richard (2002) *A History of the French New Wave Cinema* (Madison: University of Wisconsin Press).

Palmer, William J. (1993) *The Films of the 1980s* (South Illinois: Southern Illinois University Press).

Reader, Keith (1979) *Cinema: A History* (London: Hodder & Stoughton).

Rose, Al (1974) *Storyville, New Orleans* (Alabama: University of Alabama Press).

Rousso, Henry (1990) *Le Syndrome de Vichy, de 1944 à nos jours* (Paris: Editions du Seuil).

Scheers, Rob van (1997) *Paul Verhoeven* (London: Faber & Faber).

Stora, Benjamin (1991) *La Gangrène et l'oubli* (Paris: La Découverte).

Toubiana, Serge (1998) *Nouvelle vague: une légende en question*, special issue of *Cahiers du cinéma* 'Hors Série (Paris: Cahiers du cinéma).

Truffaut, François (1989) *Letters* (London: Faber & Faber).

Vine, Brian (1979) 'Pretty Tough Baby!', *Daily Express* 21 Sept.

Wiegand, Chris (2001) *French New Wave* (London: Pocket Essentials).

Williams, Alan (1992) *Republic of Images: A History of Filmmaking* (Cambridge, MA: Harvard University Press).

1 Florence Carala (Jeanne Moreau) from the opening seconds of *Ascenseur pour l' échafaud (1957)*

2 A fascist anti-hero? Alain Leroy (Maurice Ronet) in *Le Feu follet* (1963)

3 A world of despair: Alain (Maurice Ronet), the suicidal alchoholic in a scene from *Le Feu follet* (1963)

4 Louis Malle celebrates *Le Voleur*, complete with a cigar and a glass of Pernod (1966)

5 Louis Malle and Geneviève Bujold (1966). Picture from a party during the making of *Le Voleur* (1967)

6 A return to documentary film: *L' Inde fantôme* (1968)

7 Pierre Blaise as *Lacombe Lucien* (1974)

8 Lucien (Pierre Blaise), France (Aurore Clément) and Albert Horn (Holger Löwenadler) discuss the future in *Lacombe Lucien* (1974)

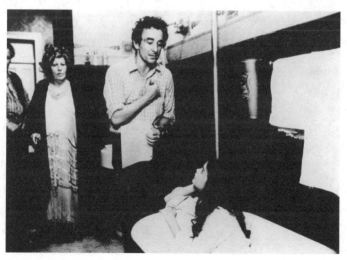

9 Malle directs Brooke Shields in *Pretty Baby* (1978)

10 Lou Paschall (Burt Lancaster) and Sally (Susan Sarandon) in *Atlantic City USA* (1980)

11 Wally (Wallace Shawn) takes a subway ... to have *My Dinner with André* (1981)

12 Glances are exchanged between Jean Bonnet (Raphaël Fejtö) and Julien Quentin (Gaspard Manesse) in *Au revoir les enfants* (1987)

2

Aesthetic vision

Critical opinion is much divided on the nature of Mallean aesthetics. On the one hand, scholars have underlined the problematic nature of identifying a single aesthetic strand in Malle's cinema. For example, Richard Roud notes: 'Malle has not obliged us by giving his films a "look" to please the customers' (1989: 125). Similarly, Pauline Kael, doyenne of film criticism, and a Malle enthusiast, finds it difficult to find unity in the oeuvre beyond what she calls a 'restless intelligence' (Kael 1975: 307). Here, then, one finds Malle the 'eclectic dilettante' rather than the systematic *auteur*. However, there is a strong case to be made that shows that Malle's films conform to a consistent aesthetic pattern that can be traced across the dramatic oeuvre. René Prédal (1989) and Jean-Pierre Colombat (1993) distinguish the classical–realist style as the defining mode through which Malle presented his fictional films. In the first part of this chapter I want to piece together the key aesthetic components that make up Malle's more general filmic grammar and to then question why despite these consistencies he remains a director who for many film scholars continues to be associated with eclecticism. Part of the answer I give to that question will highlight other traditions quite distinct from classical realism, that also feature in Malle's work. Understanding the unlikely partnership of surrealism and documentary film-making in Mallean aesthetics is important to any introduction to the director. This synthesis of film-making styles is characteristic of an artist whose work is best interpreted through its own contradictions rather than against them.

The aesthetics of Louis Malle's cinema

Although Malle contributed to a variety of genres of film (*film noir;* comedy western; heist caper; theatrical drama, to name but a few), underlying consistencies bring a sense of unity to his cinema. Throughout the fictional oeuvre, Malle repeatedly explored individual protagonists, or small groups of people, and dissected their complex inner lives and social experiences. In the course of his films, Malle's protagonists are repeatedly thrown into deep psychological flux. Malle explained the central dramatic thread that is evident in so many of his films: 'I am going to make a generalisation, even though I loathe generalisations. My films are about people who suddenly find something in their way, that diverts them from their expected path, and makes them ask themselves questions that most people manage to avoid in the course of their everyday lives' (Malle 1999: 41; Malle 1978: 51; 70). Indeed, Mallean anti-heroes as different as Alain Leroy in *Le Feu follet*, or Lou in *Atlantic City USA*, share an inability to fit in to their social environments. Suddenly, these men are forced to consider a personal revolution that changes their existence and brings major psychological disturbance. In fact, this first defining motif is especially pronounced in the several Malle films that focus on children and teenagers and their turbulent journeys to adulthood. From *Zazie dans le métro* through *Le Souffle au cœur, Lacombe Lucien, Black Moon* and *Pretty Baby* up to *Au revoir les enfants*, Malle made this territory his own.

Alongside psychological portraiture, there is a strong propensity for historical drama in Mallean cinema. Even for critics who see Malle's work as a loose patchwork this is a point of commonality in the films (Roud 1989: 126). Consistently, Malle positioned the majority of his character studies in the past. The first clearly historical drama came in Malle's sixth feature, the elaborate comedy western, *Viva Maria* (1965) set in turn of nineteenth-century Mexico. Malle returned to that critical era of the birth of the contemporary period in subsequent films *Le Voleur* (1967), *William Wilson* (1968) and *Pretty Baby* (1978). The *années noires* of collaboration, resistance and the Holocaust, the 1940s, form the second major historical focal point of the oeuvre. Films such as *Le Souffle au cœur* and *Milou en mai* stretched Malle's retrospective vision into post-war France. Importantly, Malle related his historical settings to the more focused psychological studies that he pursued: 'I'm always interested when, due to historical events, people are forced into behaviour that would not normally happen, that's created by circumstances. Suddenly people change' (Malle and French 1993: 147).

Malle's broad inclination for psychological portraiture in a historical setting marks his work as being that of a classicist. These relatively traditional subjects are the typical fare of the contemporary art house tradition. They accord exactly to the general concerns of classicism in film as defined in Colin Crisp's extensive study of the mode in its formative period, *The Classical French Cinema 1930–1960* (1993). Malle's ground is that of classical 'psychological realism' and with his fascination with historical drama he also placed himself in the tradition of the 'quality product' (Crisp 1993: xiii).

The dramatic structures that frame the content of Malle's films confirm the already classical feel of the oeuvre. Frequently, his films progress through variations on tragedy or comedy and they are structured through differentiated acts or scenes, that follow the central characters along their psychological journeys. As Prédal has noted in his analysis of *Vie privée* the style of that film is a linear one, with the narrative of Jill (Bardot)'s psychological state being charted through a tripartite structure of sub-acts that represent her past, present and future (1989: 53). And, as one would perhaps expect, the film concludes with the tragic death of its heroine. In fact, when one reviews the oeuvre, one sees that tragic or comic variations on the linear narrative structure are repeatedly employed. Films like *Le Feu follet, William Wilson, Lacombe Lucien, Au revoir les enfants* and *Damage* fall within the tradition of tragedy. *Les Amants, Zazie dans le métro, Viva Maria, Le Souffle au cœur, Atlantic City USA* and *Milou en mai* are more optimistic and function as classical comedies.

The formality of Mallean dramatic structure also points to the more general influence of literature in Malle's work (Colombat 1993: 273). In the course of his career Malle adapted several novels, including Noel Calef's *Ascenseur pour l'échafaud* (1956); Georges Darien's *Le Voleur* ([1897] 1994) Josephine Hart's *Damage* (1991) and most memorably Raymond Queneau's *Zazie dans le métro* (1959). Similarly, many of his other films offered new interpretations of original literary sources, with Malle taking a novel as a loose starting-point for his own fiction. Critical figures in the Malle library that each cast a long shadow over his thinking include: Georges Bataille, Lewis

Carroll, Anton Chekhov, Joseph Conrad, Drieu La Rochelle, F. Scott Fitzgerald, Henry James and Stendhal. The importance of each of these modernist writers for Malle marks him out as director with elite tastes, willing to rethink literature through the medium of film. This again is the world of the classicist looking to the more traditional written form for his inspiration.

Editorial style and camerawork provide significant evidence in favour of seeing Malle as a director whose work shared a common aesthetic touch, notably, a preference for realism. This is exactly the dominant visual mode one would expect to find in classical cinema and Malle consistently adopted it. Malle employed traditional cinematic techniques, combining close-ups and mid-distance shots to evoke the psychology of the characters that are displayed. Slow-paced scene-setting and smooth cutting from one scene to another add to the reassuring visual grammar. Importantly, the fundamental aim of the camera in Mallean cinema is to support the study of character or the development of plot. The camerawork displayed in Malle films is not intended to triumph over the content of the film but to render it with the utmost rigour. This is the heart of Mallean realism. In this context Malle's avowed dislike of French films of the 1990s is better understood. For Malle the younger directors were part of the MTV generation who made pictures where the camera was the star (Malle cited by Yates 1994: 24). Mallean classical realism had little time for 'filming for film's sake' let alone for the excessive meaningless stylisations of the pop video. It is worth recalling here that long before anyone had heard of MTV, Luc Besson or Jean-Jacques Beneix, Malle distinguished himself from contemporaries like Truffaut, Godard and Fellini by never making a self-reflexive film about the cinema. Reasserting his loyalty to realism Malle once joked with an audience at the British National Film Theatre that he would never make a film about the cinema because 'life' held sufficient material (1974). It is telling that Malle's only foray into the realm of depicting film-making, *Vie privée*, focused on the dilemmas of a star actress (Bardot) rather than that of a director or his or her crew.

If camerawork is used in the service of the reality of the film, many other aspects of Mallean *mise en scène* also further this objective. Through set design, prop and costume selection, audiences are immediately presented with a strong sense of time and place. This attention to detail is a further keynote in the Mallean repertoire, perhaps learned in his time working with the equally fastidious Robert Bresson on *Un condamné à mort s'est échappé*. The technique is of course of great importance in Malle's historical dramas, providing a layer of evocative contextual detail alongside psychological character-isation and narrative. Such respect for *mise en scène* was also vital to Malle's other dramatic pictures including those early films that explored his own social caste, the upper bourgeoisie. In works like *Le Feu follet* or later *Le Voleur* one is carefully drawn into a complete imaginary world that is reconstructed to appear 'real' in its own terms. Such effects were not generated by a single device but by the complete *mise en scène*, including a myriad of incidental features that combined to create the whole. As with Malle's subtle approach to the camera, the aim of the historical backdrop was to allow viewers to concentrate more easily on the psychological development of the characters within it. Malle explains the process especially well in relation to the late-nineteenth-century backdrop that was critical to *Pretty Baby*: 'yes, the period has to be as accurate as possible because then it gives you the freedom not to think about it and to look at the characters just as they are. But this means, of course, that you have a lot of homework to do in order to get to that stage ... It's interesting and troubling to sort of re-invent the past' (Malle 1979: 92).

Further supporting techniques confirm the director's preference for realism. Let us review some key examples that demonstrate a sense of recurrence in the director's work. Few Malle films experi-ment with time or use any of the common devices that disrupt filmic reality. Thus, Malle did not deploy elaborate flashbacks with any regularity. When the technique was used, as in *William Wilson*, it was executed with elegance rather than self-declamatory flamboyance. The preferred presentation of time in Mallean cinema was to follow characters through several chronologically sequential days of their lives. *Le Feu follet*, *Lacombe Lucien* or *Atlantic City USA* are each good examples of that approach. Similarly, the device of the freeze-frame was repeatedly used but only to serve as a final 'full-stop' to end a film. Voiceover is another relatively restricted device. It is employed from time to time in *Les Amants*, or to conclude *My Dinner with André*, and some years later in Malle's most personal fictional picture, *Au revoir les enfants*. More typically though, Malle's characters are left to their own devices without such God-like interventions from the director. Again consistent with classical realism, in the more mature Malle

films incidental sound was chosen over more melodramatic employ-
ment of a soundtrack. Music became an integrated feature of the
reality of the film, rather than an extraneous artistic device. This
particular technique was deployed to some effect in *Pretty Baby* where
the character of the black jazz pianist offers tunes for the brothel bar
and in so doing provides a musical soundtrack that exists inside the
reality of the film. Even the somewhat glossy *Damage* further illustrates this artistic stance. It is one of the few 'yuppie-love' movies of
the 1990s to scorn the opportunity of a commercial light rock soundtrack. Instead, Dr Fleming (Jeremy Irons) and Anna Barton (Juliette
Binoche) make love to the symbolically resonant, and authentic, sound
of the Parisian church bells of Saint-Sulpice.

By now followers of traditional *auteur* film theory, seeking patterns
in Malle's films that elevate them from run-of-the-mill genre pieces or
the frivolous interventions of a playboy sugar millionaire, will be
reassured. Beneath the superficial eclecticism of Malle's work there
are a series of aesthetic codes that distinguish his cinema from that of
his contemporaries. Such codes start to offer the personalised
signature of an artist who fulfils many of André Bazin's original
conceptions of the director as author. However, in public, at least,
Malle was never enamoured with the idea of the *auteur*. Once when
asked why he made films he replied that he could do little else.
Elaborating on this modest explanation, Malle preferred to define
himself as a *chef d'orchestre*. There is of course much to be said for this
qualification of the idea of the *auteur*. It retains Malle's shaping hand
and the recurrent artistic preoccupations of classical realism that I
have reviewed. It also has the advantage of accounting for the fact that
Malle's work was the product of a series of complex artistic collaborations.

Through his career Malle developed an evolving theatre company
of technicians to share in the experience of making films (Hawkins
1996: 33). First and foremost, at the heart of the Malle company, was
the family production business, NEF. Running a close second, Malle
shared much of his work with his long-serving editor, Suzanne
Baron. She collaborated on all Malle's films from *Le Feu follet* (1963) to
Crackers (1983). Later she was taken up by Alain Resnais to edit the
complex and playful narratives of the twin films, *Smoking/No Smoking*
(1993). Another quasi-permanent co-worker was the sound technician
Jean-Claude Laureux. His collaboration began in the 1960s when he

accompanied Malle to India to work on the documentaries *Calcutta* and *L'Inde fantôme*. This prolific partnership only ended with work on Malle's last original drama *Damage*. Camera-work and photography credits illustrate a further set of repeated, ongoing collaborations. From the early period, one must recall the prominence of cameraman Henri Decae. Later less prolific but no less important partnerships developed with Tonino Delli Colli working on *William Wilson* and *Lacombe Lucien* and Sven Nykvist contributing to *Black Moon* and *Pretty Baby*. Renato Berta worked with Malle on his last two French pictures, *Au revoir les enfants* and *Milou en mai*. Reinforcing the idea of the 'Studio Malle' approach to film, the preferred working method that developed over the years was the use of a small crew, preferably less than twenty. This economy of size facilitated a fast pace in shooting time, which Malle preferred when filming.

Whether one interprets Malle as a forgotten *auteur*, or a *chef d'orchestre*, it remains important to question why his work is so often perceived by film critics as eclectic or lacking a defining artistic mode. There are of course many answers to the question. Malle's unique biographical background and his emigration to the United States contribute to the perception that he was a cinematic gadfly, flitting from one project to another. An alternative explanation is that the controversial subjects Malle filmed concealed his own work behind the camera and with Suzanne Baron in the editing suite. However, a more complex explanation can be added that relates directly to the very nature of Malle's realism.

In 1984, the British Broadcasting Company's prestigious arts documentary series, Arena, devoted a feature-length programme to Malle. Produced by Alan Yentob, *My Dinner with Louis* brought together the director and his friend 'Wally' Shawn for conversation over lunch in a downtown Atlantic City restaurant. In scenes that were deliberately reminiscent of their film, *My Dinner with André*, they mused over the many projects that Malle had completed since his arrival on the international film scene in the 1950s. Here, Malle explained to Wally what he saw as his fundamental position concerning the cinema. Exuding the complete confidence of a French intellectual at the height of his powers, Malle told Shawn: 'the best definition of what I do is Stendhal's definition of a novel: "it's just walking alongside a road with a mirror' ... the mirror being the camera ... it works very well for my interest in film-making' (Shawn and Malle in Yentob 1984). The director did not elaborate further on a remark that on first hearing sounds straightforward enough but that one later realises is truly a subtle and intriguing metaphor for his aesthetic pose. Malle's central artistic aim was to offer films that provided closed, credible, imaginative versions of reality, mirror-like reflections of the world he explored. The spirit of the Mallean mirror was to generate an artistic reality that not only imagined a coherent fictional world but also deployed every strategy possible to conceal the 'mirror' itself – which is after all the intrinsic quality of a perfect mirror. I think that it is for this reason that Malle has so often been taken as an unsystematic or even a failed director. The fundamental aspect of Mallean aesthetics that has been too often overlooked by critics is Malle's desire to achieve a level of realism that renders his own work invisible. Paradoxically, many of the features of Malle's aesthetic approach that I have raised to demonstrate continuity and recurrence, his potential *auteurship* if one accepts that now long disputed theory, were executed to conceal this very notion, to hide the director's hand behind the realist content of his work. In Mallean film the common, abiding objective is realism. It was critical for Malle that his technique, his direction, should not stand out, or call itself forth, for critical evaluation. For it to do so would immediately remind audiences that they were watching 'a Louis Malle film' and not a work of meticulous realist fiction.

General philosophical tendencies in Malle's approach to film support my characterisation of Malle as a self-effacing *auteur*. Directorial distance and a neutrality of tone were especially important to Malle. While frequently filming periods of controversial political history, Malle did not think of his work as being a vehicle for direct political persuasion or propaganda. This would have lacked subtlety and started to break the central illusion of realism. Should too overt a political message be pursued, then the work would simply become a platform for Malle's opinions and thus jeopardise its realism. This aspect of his work was reflected onscreen by what Malle called his preference for 'showing' rather than 'instructing'. As Malle explained in the late 1970s: 'On dérange plus en montrant qu'en démontrant' (Malle 1978: 39; 70). Importantly, Malle never denied the potential political meaning of any of his projects but he was careful not to let his works fall into *films à thèse*. Any such move would have compromised the dominant tendency that I am illustrating.

Malle's approach to casting is equally telling. This critical aspect of the film-making process was of utmost importance for Malle because he felt that the choice of actors and actresses for a film could either bring greater integrity to the internal realism of the picture or completely break it. Malle took great care over his casting decisions, often looking far and wide for appropriate actors with appropriate faces for the parts. Malle once even remarked that successful casting represented 90 per cent of the director's task (cited in Camber Porter 1993: 24). Ultimately, actors were often selected by Malle on the basis of a desire to balance the use of well-known classical performers with less well-known younger players who were often new to the cinema. Malle was prepared to use stars but was deeply aware that their misuse would jeopardise the realism he consistently sought (Malle 1974b; Malle cited in Johnstone 1990: 12). After all, there was little point devoting such attention to classical photography and historically plausible realism, *mise en scène*, if suddenly a world-famous film personality dominated the frame. Likewise, should Malle's work become too closely associated with one star then his careful strategy of directorial self-effacement would be compromised, the film too quickly becoming a Malle–Belmondo or a Malle–Delon venture.

Of course, in his more commercial films Malle did use stars, notably, Moreau and Bardot in the star-vehicle film, *Viva Maria*. But, far more commonly, he combined recognised film actors and actresses with other lesser-known players, international actors willing to work in French cinema, or first-time performers. In films like *Lacombe Lucien*, *Atlantic City USA*, or *Milou en mai*, British, German, Swedish, Canadian and Italian actors were all used alongside French or American cast members. The deployment of children or teenage actors proved to be a major advantage to achieve the Malle vision of ur-realism. These new cinematic faces were not associated with previous performances. In that sense they were 'real' characters and would appear convincing to audiences, being known only in the context of Malle's film. Brilliant performances were often achieved through this approach: most notably that of Pierre Blaise in *Lacombe Lucien*. Blaise had been cast for the part of Lucien only after some 651 previous auditions from other young hopefuls (Cognacq 2001: 42).

To illustrate Malle's casting strategy and his fidelity to realism further *Le Souffle au cœur* is a fine example. For that film Malle cast the well-known French star Daniel Gélin, the Italian actress, Lea

Massari and the teenage unknowns, Benoît Ferreux, François Werner and Liliane Sorval. This combination achieved the realistic look Malle wanted for his light comedy on incest and the bourgeoisie. Despite the ultimately shocking theme, Malle used his casting to create a plausible family, the members of which would not look like a group of actors but rather a snapshot of the middle-class home. By drawing on a variety of talents, foreign actors, a French star and first-time child performers, realism was defended.

Turning to issues behind the screen rather than on it, Mallean realism also concealed Malle the film producer. Malle's commercial interests in French cinema were extensive and over the years the Malle family was to become a key commercial force, with NEF colleagues negotiating international coproduction financing and acquiring a small chain of French art cinemas (Billard 2003: 305–6). To illustrate the connections Malle achieved in the wider international film community, including in the United States, it is sufficient to recall two symbolically indicative episodes. In the early 1970s Malle was charged with organising the French-language edition of Francis Ford Coppola's epic, *The Godfather* (1972). Peter Cowie takes up the story:

> Bludhorn and Evans [of Paramount/CIC] talked with Malle and offered him half a million francs to supervise the dubbing. Malle bypassed the usual pool of actors who specialized in dubbing American pictures and chose instead respected players such as Michel Duchaussoy (Don Coreleone) Claude Dauphin (Woltz) and newcomer Sylvain Joubert (Michael) ... within a matter of weeks [of opening] *The Godfather* had become the largest-grossing Hollywood film of all time in France. (1997: 72–3)

Malle's ability to participate in this project is a striking illustration of the profile he was to achieve as an artist *and* as a multitalented cinema impresario. However, Malle was not always able to win the projects he was interested in. A second episode is equally telling. Controversy continues to surround Malle's interest in filming another major Hollywood project, *The Killing Fields*. Pierre Billard contends that Malle turned down the opportunity to direct this important picture (2003: 458). However, a respected biography of David Puttnam, the British producer of *The Killing Fields*, brings different insights to a fascinating case of Hollywood infighting. Andrew Yule reports that Malle, Puttnam and *The Killing Fields* scriptwriter, Bruce Robinson met to discuss the putative film. However, Robinson was horrified by

Malle's plans, recalling: 'I couldn't believe what this fucker was saying. He's talking about ballets of B52s in the opening sequence' (cited in Yule 1988: 223). Following this encounter Puttnam remained loyal to his original scriptwriter and had the task of rejecting Malle. Yule takes up the story: 'In turning Malle down, David wrote to the ubiquitous Sam Cohn, who also just happened to be Malle's agent, saying, "Bruce's script to which I am heavily committed, has gone too far to be turned around and made into what could be termed a Louis Malle film"' (Puttnam cited in Yule: 224). This episode is instructive for several reasons. It confirms Malle's status in the United States, with Puttnam having to take a brave decision to side with the little heard of scriptwriter Robinson. It also highlights the figure of Malle's one-time agent in the United States, Sam Cohn. Like the dubbing of *The Godfather*, it recalls that behind the illusory realism of his films Malle was fully engaged in the occasionally grubby routine of the commercial film business.

Malle was anything but a dilettante. Simply, the very qualities of his classical realism privileged his films over his reputation as an *auteur*, let alone the more commercially sensitive side of film production. From time to time Malle did use overtly filmic techniques (voiceovers/sound/freeze-frames) but they were predominantly deployed to tell the story of the film, to enhance understanding of its characters or setting, rather than to parade their director's cinematic prowess. So, if one accepts the theoretical premise, Malle *is* just as much an *auteur* as a Truffaut, a Chabrol or a Losey. However, a persuasive explanation as to why this status was never consistently sought by Malle, nor fully granted by the critics, is that his work actively undermined this reading. Malle's version of *auteur* cinema was attenuated by his desire to produce work that would function with complete internal integrity. Malle was correct to define himself modestly as a '*chef d'orchestre*' but in fact his dominant aesthetic mode highlights something far more challenging: a self-effacing *auteur*.

Mallean surrealism

Malle's classical realism did not function to the exclusion of other traditions or techniques. An important further element of Malle's interpretation of classicism was his openness to more experimental and *avant-garde* methods. The two most important contributory currents to his classicism were: surrealism and documentary. The influence of these traditions on Malle's work further explain why so often in the past his cinema has seemed too diverse, too difficult for critics to pin down or to theorise. Yet, remarkably, as I will explain the currents within Malle's work more often than not achieved a powerful synthesis in his films.

The first signs of the importance of surrealism in the oeuvre were demonstrated in Malle's decision in the late 1950s to adapt Raymond Queneau's *Zazie dans le métro*. Queneau, an ex-surrealist and ex-Marxist, had become a literary hit after publishing the novel on which the film was based (1959). It is the simple story of the misadventures of the rumbustious and frequently cursing Zazie's first visit to Paris. Swearing and shouting her way through the city, she is obsessed with her mission to take a ride on the métro. Malle's approach to filming this well-known instant literary success were in strong contrast to his previous two films. In narrating a little girl's crazy experience of a weekend in Paris, Malle demonstrated an enormous range of cinematic techniques and styles. Some years later describing the film as 'byzantine', Malle recalled the various techniques he had tested out when making *Zazie* (Malle and French 1993: 26–9). These included eight and twelve frame-per-second photography; slow-motion acting; mirrored background effects in two-handed scenes; collapsing sets; as well as numerous other destabilising effects. The result is a truly unique filmic collage that does not leave the viewer more than a second to catch breath before a new visual style is demonstrated. Here, then, Malle was working in an aesthetic tradition far removed from that demonstrated in later more classical work like *Le Souffle au cœur* or *Au revoir les enfants*. In adapting *Zazie* to the cinema Malle defined his profile in 1959 as being approximate to the modernist New Novel, an experimental tradition that in literature was far removed from Mallean classicism (cited in Chapier 1964: 32).

Zazie dans le métro is a reminder of the difficulties of defining the Malle style with reference exclusively to classical realism.[1] Indeed, in

1 An alternative, less obvious, starting point for this discussion might well also be found in *Ascenseur pour l'échafaud*. While the dominant genre is *film noir* Malle's film also displays more than the occasional hint of surrealism. Not least in terms of plot: the man trapped in the lift, the woman left alone to wander the streets of a deserted Paris, the wrong murder being committed by the wrong murderer.

the light of that film one is more sympathetic to the view that Malle 'does not seem to have any single identifiable style' (Hawkins 1996: 30). Nevertheless, *Zazie* announced a new element of consistency that was slowly married to classical realism: a long-term, recurrent admiration for surrealism. For example, filming in Buñuel's Mexico, *Viva Maria* finds much of its humour in its all too brief glimpses of surrealist detail. Later, in the United States, Malle's 'flop', *Crackers*, featured passages of a similar style. Another later film, *Milou en mai* draws extensively on fantasy, especially with its concluding coda in which Milou (Piccoli) and the ghost of his dead mother (Paulette Dubost) dance a last waltz together. However, it was in 1975 in making *Black Moon* that Malle's most substantial engagement with surrealism was executed. *Black Moon* is an atypical Malle picture in its ahistorical science fiction setting. Loosely based on Lewis Carroll's *Alice in Wonderland*, Malle filmed a fantasy world of unicorns, talking rats and Indian mythology. In a profoundly surrealist move, Malle was offering audiences nothing less than a film of his dreams (Malle and French 1993: 106–7). This idea had always been a core objective of surrealist cinema in the 1930s, and despite Malle's many other differences from that group, he is one of the few film-makers to have actually executed just such a utopian project.

Furthermore, in an intriguing and complex piece of writing the philosopher Gilles Deleuze identifies a dream-like quality across much of Mallean cinema (1989: 60). Deleuze sees Mallean film as an oeuvre in which the fictional characters are secondary to the forces of the cinematic world in which they live. This facet of Malle's work produces an aesthetic close to the experience of the dream. Deleuze explains: 'there takes place a kind of worldizing or societizing, a depersonalizing ... the frightened child faced with danger cannot run away, but the world sets about running for him' (59). Applying this theoretical description more closely to Malle, Deleuze continues:

> From *Ascenseur pour l'échafaud* onwards it was the halting of the lift which blocked the murderer's movement, to put in its place

---

Like the work of Hitchcock, Malle's first feature thus anticipates David Lynch's more elaborate syntheses of *film noir* and surrealism, *Blue Velvet* (1987), *Lost Highway* (1997) and *Mulholland Drive* (2001). While Lynch has developed this aesthetic, also incorporating his fascination with Americana, no French director has systematically applied the style to a European setting.

movements of a world involving the other characters. The culmination is *Black Moon*, where the depersonalized movement takes the heroine with the unicorn from one world to still another. It is by running away from the initial images of violence that the heroine moves from one world to the other, in the sense that Sartre says that each dream is a world, and even each phase or image a dream. (60)

The interpretation is fascinating and throws a powerful sidelight on Malle's work. As I suggested above, Mallean cinema does emphasise the creation of complete, discrete, often historical 'worlds' in which central characters struggle for their survival while all around them the rules of the game are shifting against them. Nonetheless, it remains a moot point as to whether Mallean characterisation leaves the protagonists as completely helpless or dreamlike as Deleuze implies. I think that the psychological realism of Malle's films, its emphasis on character, leaves some autonomy of action, but, one might add, not always a great deal.

Beyond the question of the dream, Malle's interest in surrealism seeps into his wider approach to cinema. In particular, his repeated focus on episodes of human irrationality and emotional turmoil frequently also draw him towards that aesthetic and political tradition. In their study *Les Surréalistes et le cinéma*, Alain and Odette Virmaux define surrealist film's main thematic ground as being, 'revolt, dreams and love' (1976: 89) and Malle's work shares these concerns in abundance. Furthermore, as Buñuel explains, the surrealist project was founded on the power to shock and provoke scandal. Looking back in his memoirs (a work co-authored by Jean-Claude Carrière), he recalled:

although the surrealists didn't consider themselves terrorists, they were constantly fighting a society they despised. Their principal weapon wasn't guns, of course, it was scandal. Scandal was a potent agent of revelation, capable of exposing such social crimes as the exploitation of one man by another, colonialist imperialism, religious tyranny – in sum all the secret and odious underpinnings of a system that had to be destroyed. (1994: 107)

In many respects the passage describes much which is true of Malle's approach to film after May '68. In particular films like *Le Souffle au cœur* and *Lacombe Lucien* very much fit this bill. They too sought to overturn dominant discourses and conventions and were founded on the power of provocation. The surrealists' traditional anti-clericalism was also taken up by Malle on several occasions. Noting in his memoirs that he lost any religious faith when a teenager (Malle 1978: 13), his filmic world includes several penetrating attacks on the Church, many of which could be directly lifted from a Buñuel picture. In *Viva Maria*, the two Marias (Bardot and Moreau) wage a terrorist war against a corrupt priest who is waspishly mocked by Malle throughout the film. Thus, at the end of that film the priest's head is blown off, and subsequently it is caught by the still functioning body. Some years later, in *Le Souffle au cœur* Malle offered a darker glimpse of Church education in provincial France of the 1950s. Long before its central character makes love with his mother (actually proving to be a happy turn of events for the family), he is shown to be the object of illicit desire of one of his Catholic schoolmasters. In fact, in that otherwise comic film about incest, Michel Lonsdale's cameo part as Father Henry represents a genuinely sinister side to growing up in 1950s Dijon. Later, elements of *Au revoir les enfants* continued this line of reasoning, although that film also shows that some members of the Church were capable of great bravery in the service of the anti-fascist struggle.

As well as the more or less directly surreal film projects (*Zazie*; *Black Moon*) and the shared thematic ground with surrealism, the fundamental look of passages of Malle's cinema gained from lessons drawn from the tradition. Here, I think the best and most prominent illustration is found in Malle's most widely discussed film *Lacombe Lucien*. The extended sequences that form the first section of *Lacombe Lucien* are shot in a relatively loose narrative style, departing from Malle's usual classical narration and conventional use of montage. Instead, the viewer is treated to a sequence of loosely connected episodes from Lucien's life. The montaging used is not that of classical cinema but far closer to the disturbing symbolism associated with surrealism. Malle presents Lucien hunting, slurping his soup, bloodily executing a chicken with his bare hands, and so on. In the midst of this depiction of everyday rural violence, a church procession marches incongruously over a sunburnt hillside, an elaborate crucifix to the fore. These rituals of Christian civilisation are strangely out of place in this most verdant corner of Nazi-occupied France. Later, in scenes that hint at the surrealists' attraction for putrefaction and dead animals, the farmers who live alongside Lucien drag a dead horse across the yard. Despite the violence and shadow of death, faint evening sunlight filters the rustic scenery and offers a strangely poetic air. The combined impact of these passages from the film is to disorient the viewer. Lucien's later pro-Nazi collaboration arrives only after the audience has been symbolically prepared for this political transgression by the surrealist look of the extended introduction that I describe. These sequences, and several others in Malle's best-known work of the 1970s, show how the surrealist aesthetic blended into the otherwise classical–realist framework.

Like so many other French upper-class intellectuals Malle was attracted to the avant-garde, becoming a curious and intelligent reader of Queneau, Boris Vian (another friend with 1950s impeccable surrealist credentials), the anarchist Georges Darien, as well as later the unclassifiable Georges Bataille. Malle was a close friend of Luis Buñuel, and some time collaborator with his son Jean-Luis. Their mutual friend, Jean-Claude Carrière worked on scripts for both men. These connections alone indicate how it is difficult to understand Malle without addressing the wider *avant garde* tradition in general, and surrealism in particular. In retrospect, the synthesis of commercial classicism and experimental surrealism might seem an impossible *rendez-vous* but bringing contradictions together was often the way Malle worked. In some films – like *Zazie dans le métro* or *Black Moon* – the experimental side won out and was the dominant mode. In other features, classical realism dominated and surrealist touches were kept within the parameters of the dominant realism of the project. However, even in filming as conventional a comedy drama as *Milou en mai* Malle borrowed and fused elements from the two traditions. A sense of surrealist irony is to be found across his films. One can take the director at his word when he reported that his work contained a sense of wickedness that is indebted to Buñuel (Malle 1979: 94).

The synthesis of classical realism and surrealism in Mallean aesthetics I have analysed underlines the fact that Malle's work again refutes over-schematic discussion. To illustrate the point by using a negative comparison, no director could be further from the famous 1990s Danish directors' *Dogme* code of film-making practice than Louis Malle. I think Malle would have loathed *Dogme* theory because of its initial wager: that one must make films in line with a pre-established cinematic rulebook that was overtly revealed for all to see.

Unlike *Dogme* realism, Mallean realism, or Mallean surrealism, were generated through as many appropriate techniques as possible. For Malle each new project offered a story to tell and it was his duty to execute the film to the best of his ability. If this meant marshalling relatively classical techniques, so be it. On the other hand, if a more experimental, *avant-garde*, or surreal perspective was of help to the film then that too was woven into its fabric by Malle. It is also for this reason that Mallean aesthetics confound structuralist film analysis on the nature of realism (McCabe 1974). Importantly, Malle's cinema does not offer a single stable version of realism to theorise. Instead, the key elements McCabe identified in realism: narrative (the metalanguage, the real) and character (the overtly fictive) are scrambled. Malle's emphasis on the narrative importance of the psychology of his characters blurs any distinction between character and narrative, in the way Deleuze's comments on the dreamlike qualities of Mallean film earlier implied. Moreover, the introduction of surrealism to the films adds to the difficulties Malle presents for structuralist film analysis. Malle did not make films in which there is a 'surreal' element neatly counter-pointed to a realist discourse. Instead, as I have illustrated in films like *Lacombe Lucien* the two categories tend to overlap, with no clear distinction as to which form is reliant on the other. In fact, a remarkably successful balance was achieved in Malle's best work.

Cinéma direct: documentary film

Malle's documentary work provides a further major influence on his fictional output. Major projects like *L'Inde fantôme*, *Humain, trop humain*, or the later American films *God's Country* and *And the Pursuit of Happiness*, form a critical strand of Malle's career. Since it would be inappropriate to read Malle's substantial contributions to the documentary exclusively in the light of his fiction, let us first recall the more general qualities of his work in this field before relating them to Malle's approach to fiction.

The seven major documentaries that Malle directed are all forms of travelogue journalism. Broadly, this is as true for his first work with Cousteau on *Le Monde du silence*, as it is for his own major television documentary series on India or the two documentaries devoted to life in the United States. At first glance Malle's French-based documentaries, *Place de la République* and *Humain, trop humain* are exceptions to the rule. Yet, they too have similar investigative and journalistic qualities. These films focus on subjects far removed from Malle's experience of his homeland: the automotive industry and working-class Parisian street life. The central hook on which all the documentaries hang is Malle's engagement with the material that he finds 'on the road' or, as in *Place de la République*, literally on the street corner. At different stages of his life Malle saw himself not only as a director but also as a roving journalist, flying away from Paris to capture a breaking news event. This was the case in 1956 when he attempted to reach Budapest to film scenes of the Soviet suppression of the anti-Communist uprising, for instance (Chapier 1964: 62; Malle 1978: 17). Later, during the French war of decolonisation in Algeria he embarked on a further news expedition (recorded in travel notes published in Malle 1978: 93–102). It is very much in the spirit of these first attempts at reportage that Malle later produced his major documentary films. In this way, at the beginning of *God's Country* Malle excitedly comments, 'Un samedi de juin, il y a quelques années, et nous voilà – une petite ville de middle-west en train de faire quelques amis. Deux semaines encore nous avons filmé le Minnesota par hasard de rencontre. J'étais heureux de prendre la route, encore caméra à la main'.[2]

Malle has described his philosophy and method of documentary film-making as being part of the *cinéma direct* school (1988). This is the form of documentary that emphasises its proximity to real life, exploring human experiences as directly as is possible through the lens of a camera and the assistance of a handheld microphone. As Gilles Marsolais has explained in his study of the method, the critical emphasis is for the film-maker to capture live social experiences (1974: 22) and for their cinema to be one that 'works on the ground'. Philosophically, and practically, the *cinéma direct* school privileges the idea of communication between the film-maker and the world he or she is filming (Marsolais 1974: 22). While not claiming to be any more truthful than any other form of mediated visual material, *cinéma*

2 A Saturday in June, a few years ago and here we are in a little mid-west town in the course of making friends. For a further two weeks we filmed Minnesota on the basis of chance encounters. I was happy to be on the road, with the camera in my hands again.'

direct implies a greater proximity to lived experience because of its simple, open and communicative approach. The technique was commonly applied in post-war documentary in America, Canada and France, with a period of some popularity coming between 1958 and 1965 (Marsolais 1974: 99), coincidentally close to Malle's own visit to India and first experiment with the method. Among the better-known exponents of *cinéma direct* are the American film journalists, Richard Leacock, Robert Drew, Alan Pennebaker and Albert Maysles. In French television it is associated with the work of Michel Brault and Georges Dufaux (Marsolais 1974: 121). Probably the best-known documentary maker to occasionally work with *cinéma direct* is Chris Marker. He contributed to the idea of *cinéma direct* in *Cuba si* (1962) and to an extent in his film on contemporary Paris, *Le Joli Mai* (1963) (Marsolais 1974: 187–90).

For Malle a defining work of *cinéma direct* is his own *Place de la République* (1974). Malle, soundman Laureux and cameraman Etienne Becker, spent eight days filming on the famous Parisian square. From this footage of everyday life, and the community's own reaction to the presence of a film crew asking questions of them, an instant picture of the district is offered. This is a quintessential *cinéma direct* approach to documentary. Although the location and therefore general subject matter is selected in advance by Malle, the content of the raw footage is entirely determined by the events that develop at the time of filming. Malle summarises:

> Le cinéma direct est un cinéma de l'instantané, un travail d'improvisation constante, et les choix se font constamment à la caméra. La mise en scene donc, dans la mesure où elle est constituée d'une serie de choix, mais on les fait sur le moment. Après, on se demande, au montage, pourquoi on les fait sur le moment. (Malle 1988: 24)[3]

Many of his other documentaries confirm a fidelity to this method of work. All his documentaries were researched but they were in no way scripted or prepared in the way one might storyboard a fictional drama (Malle 1988: 22). As with *Place de la République* the shooting

3 '*Cinéma Direct* is a cinema of the instantaneous, a work of constant improvisation, where the choices are made constantly by the camera. Therefore, the *mise en scène* is constituted by a series of choices, but they are made at the moment of filming. Afterwards, one asks oneself, during the editing, why you did it that way, at that time.'

was an improvised process that was freeflowing, determined by events on the ground and the amount of film available to use. The India experience is illustrative of the technique as pursued by Malle. Malle and his minimal crew travelled and shot across India for several weeks, returning to Paris to try to edit together a film of that experience. The result of hours of raw film was just nine hours of finished material subdivided into two projects, *Calcutta* and the *L'Inde fantôme* television series. The editing of the project took Malle and Suzanne Baron one year, or as Malle reported, 'another year in India' (Malle 1978: 33) Even in the far more restricted project *God's country* Malle notes that the editing of hours of direct footage took six months to complete (Malle 1988: 22).

Malle exploited the emphasis of *cinéma direct* on film as a medium of communication between director and subject. Malle saw this quality in his own work, describing his documentaries as sudden intrusions into other people's experiences. The very act of filming allowed him to be closer to different people and social milieu than would otherwise have been the case. It is this immediacy of contact that Malle identified as another critical element of his documentaries. Just as people respond to journalists, Malle has noted that quick but intimate relationships are established because of the presence of the camera. On the one hand, for the interviewee it is an opportunity to speak, to tell their story. On the other hand, for the director and camera crew it is not only an opportunity to listen and record material but also to capture the visual impact of this encounter as it is transformed into celluloid. For Malle *cinéma direct* held the potential to explore: 'Toutes les contradictions qu'on peut lire, la façon dont ils bougent, dont ils parlent, leurs silences, la difficulté de certains mots, certaines phrases' (Malle 1988: 25).[4]

Malle's documentaries follow much that was learned from *cinéma direct*. They also developed a unique style of their own that does not wholly conform to the wider tradition. The use of narrative voiceovers from Malle are perhaps their definitive feature, and one that is some way apart from notions of rigorous direct film-making. In bold contrast to Malle's limited use of voiceover in his fiction, Malle is an ever-present participant in most of his major documentaries. In this

4 'All the contradictions that one can read, the way they move, the way they speak, the way they are silent, the difficulties of certain words, certain phrases.'

field he was often the 'star' of his own films. The strategy began with
L'Inde fantôme and here Malle used his own position as an outsider in
India to frame the series of films (Gitlin 1974). Malle's later handling
of America in *God's Country* and *And the Pursuit of Happiness* follows
the technique developed in India. However, a notable exception to the
voiceover technique was *Humain, trop humain*. The study of the industrial process as carried out in the Citroën factory, Rennes, did not
invite extended commentary from Malle. That film spoke for itself.

How did Mallean *cinéma direct* contribute to the aesthetic strategies
executed in his fictional works? In Malle's own mind the two forms
were closely related professional experiences. Throughout his career
Malle exchanged one form of film-making for another and used this
change of professional experience to remain fresh and intrigued
about the challenges of cinema. As I underlined in the previous
chapter, *L'Inde fantôme* provided Malle with an outlet for his ideas and
emotions just when his fictional work had reached a crisis point after
Le Voleur and *William Wilson*. Repetitious studio work on *Le Voleur*
was replaced with the excitement of the journey to India, the first
experiments with shooting *cinéma direct*. Similarly, following two
fictional box-office failures in the United States, *Crackers* and *Alamo
Bay*, Malle completed his documentary *God's Country*. Returning to
the documentary again served as a personal release after minor
commercial misfortune (Malle and Ezine 1986). Documentary offered
Malle a sabbatical away from the demands of commercial cinema. It
offered Malle a different way of making pictures that in turn
prompted new fictional projects. Malle's best-known works, *Le Souffle
au cœur*, *Lacombe Lucien* and *Au revoir les enfants*, each followed
documentary-film experiments.

The most obvious link between Mallean classicism and the techniques of *cinéma direct* is their shared emphasis on the real. On the
one hand, in his fiction Malle wanted to convey a completely plausible
sense of reality. On the other hand, in the documentaries Malle was
working with a technique that sought to capture reality with as much
immediacy as possible. The intellectual and practical consistency
between the two ambitions is self-evident. The theory and practice of
cinéma direct offered a model and a method that could be applied to
enrich fictional drama. However, as with the influence of surrealism
it was rarely deployed to the extent of compromising Malle's more
general leaning to his own self-effacing classicism.

More practically speaking, in the light of *cinéma direct* Malle developed an increasingly improvisational style of directing actors. By the mature period of his career he wanted to treat the experience of working with actors as being comparable to filming documentaries where in unrehearsed *cinéma direct* productions everything is subject to improvisation. In particular, the almost instant intimacy that documentary film-making could bring between director and subject was something that Malle increasingly sought to replicate in his handling of fiction (Malle cited in Prédal 1989: 90). Further lessons from documentary film gradually informed Malle's creative modus operandi. Documentary handheld camerawork and direct sound recording were both used in the making of *Lacombe Lucien* and add considerably to that film (Prédal 1989: 96). These techniques had been practised throughout the shooting of the Indian films, and Malle was familiar with what could be achieved in the light of that experience.

Probably the most significant and prolonged interplays between fiction and documentary in Malle's work are to be found in the films he made in the United States. Malle's five American fictions and two documentaries closely overlap in their tone and overall subject matter. Each of Malle's American fictional films are explorations of place, ranging from New Orleans (*Pretty Baby*) and Port Alamo (*Alamo Bay*) in the South, to Atlantic City and New York in the north-east (*Atlantic City USA* and *My Dinner with André*), and Los Angeles (*Crackers*) on the west coast. This thematic development clearly originates in Malle's long-held self-identity as a journalistic film-maker, travelling from location to location in search of a story and images through which to tell it. Furthermore, the two documentaries Malle made in the United States continued where the fiction left off. Whereas *Atlantic City USA* took on the subject of that decaying seaside resort, *God's Country* offered a snapshot of life in a small-town rural community of the mid-west. Given the level of thematic similarity, one is not surprised to discover that *Alamo Bay* had been first intended as a documentary project (Malle and French 1993: 148). In fact, Malle arrived too late in Texas to film racial tensions as they occurred and so instead decided to tackle the subject through realist fiction.

Notwithstanding the provenance of *Alamo Bay*, *My Dinner with André* is the Malle drama that is most clearly influenced by documentary and in particular the earlier film, *Place de la République*. The common point of departure is that both these films are composed entirely of human speech. Whereas Malle invited passersby to speak to camera in the documentary, the fictional piece captured the extended dinner table debate between the actor and the theatrical director. Indeed, one might profitably speculate that part of Malle's interest in *My Dinner with André* was derived from his positive experience of filming a similar subject in the earlier documentary. Indeed, the opening passages of the drama that follow Wally to the restaurant in downtown Manhattan readily recall the edginess of street life Malle had captured in Paris. Moreover, in the visual composition of the conversation that takes place between Shawn and André Gregory, Malle achieves a cinematic look that many viewers imagine was a product of a single improvised documentary-style take. Thus, the look of the film is just the informality of conversation Malle had previously captured in *Place de la République*.

In fact, Shawn and Gregory's conversation was systematically reconstructed through an extended period of rehearsal and broken shooting (Malle and French 1993: 137). Although the look of the film was *cinéma direct*, the method of its shooting was the inverse. Malle had achieved the semblance of freeflowing dialogue through numerous instrumental cuts between speeches from the two men. *My Dinner with André* is a dramatic, very indirect, fantasy of *cinéma direct*. As such it is the Malle film that is most influenced by the director's contributions to documentary. While *Alamo Bay* was inspired by the idea of a documentary film on a similar journalistic subject, *My Dinner with André* recaptured the style of *cinéma direct* through the methods of realist fictional film-making. Such an ambitious project would not have been possible without Malle's deep knowledge of the documentary form. It is the high watermark of Malle's use of documentary in his fiction. It is a defining reminder that Mallean classical realism was inevitably influenced by his work in documentary. Indeed, there is also more than a touch of surrealism, a hint of Samuel Beckett's theatre of the absurd, in the film's wager that one can shoot a work exclusively about a two hour conversation over a three-course meal.

Conclusion: 'Personally, I think I tend to repeat myself ...' [5]

Malle's remark to Philip French is another witty aside, cast in the direction of those critics who repeatedly overemphasised his eclecticism. It is true that among his contemporaries Malle demonstrated a far greater range of film-making strategies and aesthetic priorities than most. In a career of cross-genre film-making and frequent movements between fiction and documentary, the critical route of least resistance is to see Malle as a brilliant dilettante. However, as I have suggested in this chapter, significant patterns of aesthetic consistency emerge over a career that show that a self-effacing *auteur/ chef d'orchestre* was at work. The dominant mood is classical realism and the most common additional contributory currents to that aesthetic choice are derived from the surrealism and the bold realism of *cinéma direct*. Confounding over-schematic theories of film-making, these tributaries are not mutually exclusive artistic currents. In Malle's cinema they share a common preference for spontaneity and an eye for detail. It is perhaps the complex synthesis of all three aesthetic traditions that makes Mallean cinema a unique cultural form that has not been easily mimicked by others. It is also perhaps the complexity of this synthesis that has led Malle to fall outside the cannonic writings of film theory.

There is no pure example of Mallean film that displays every core aspect of his aesthetic, or that captures everything that is typical in one place. Such a film would be ludicrous. Nonetheless, poignantly, Malle's final film to be made in France contains more Mallean touches than most. *Milou en mai* gathers together much evidence of the strategies that we have discussed in this chapter. Like so many Malle films it is closely related to a literary source (Anton Chekhov's *The Cherry Orchard*). Furthermore, in its exploration of one family's experiences of the *événements* of May '68 it combines a powerful fusion of historical context with psychological characterisation. If one looks closely again at the film, *Milou en mai* also combines strong touches of surrealism and *cinéma direct*. Surrealist images are frequently hinted at in the comic encounters between the different family members and the utopian mood inspired by May '68. Similarly, sometimes controversial ground, the ageing Milou's fascination with his young granddaughter, is hinted at with a certain wickedness (and sexism)

5 Malle and French 1993: 208.

reminiscent of *Black Moon* and more obviously, *Le Souffle au cœur* and *Pretty Baby*. *Cinéma direct* is less obviously a feature here. But, its influence is ever present in Malle's attention to authentic reconstruction of historical detail in the film, his loyalty to the integral realism of the film.

In a purely technical sense of learning about Mallean aesthetics, *Milou en mai* is a good place to continue reviewing the oeuvre. That film alone will not resolve the eternal debate of 'eclecticism versus consistency' in Mallean aesthetics, but it does lend considerable weight to the side of the argument that I have pursued. Indeed, if debating Malle the self-effacing *auteur* presents its own critical challenges, the tensions here are less marked than those to which we will now turn regarding the political status of the early part of Malle's oeuvre that dates from the late 1950s.

References

Billard, Pierre (2003) *Louis Malle: Le Rebelle solitaire* (Paris: Plon).

Buñuel, Luis (1994) *My Last Breath* (London: Vintage).

Calef, Noel (1956) *Ascenseur pour l'échafaud* (Paris: Fayard).

Camber Porter, Melinda (1993) 'Louis Malle Talks to Melinda Camber Porter about *Damage*', *The Times* (24 January), 24.

Chapier, Henri (1964) *Louis Malle* (Paris: Seghers).

Cognacq, Maud (2001) '*Lacombe Lucien* et Louis Malle: portrait d'un film au regard de l'histoire', MA dissertation; supervised by Olivier Dumoulin, Lettres et Sciences Humaines, University of Rouen.

Colombat, André Pierre (1993) *The Holocaust in French Film* (London: Scarecrow Press).

Cowie, Peter (1997) *The Godfather Book* (London: Faber & Faber).

Crisp, Colin (1993) *The Classic French Cinema 1930–1960* (Bloomington: Indiana University Press).

Darien, Georges ([1897] 1994) *Le Voleur* (Paris: Seuil).

Deleuze, Gilles (1989) *Cinema 2: The Time-Image* (London: The Athlone Press).

Gitlin, Todd (1974) 'Phantom India', *Film Quarterly* 27.4: 57–60.

Hart, Jospehine (1991) *Damage* (London: Chatto & Windus).

Hawkins, Peter (1996) 'Louis Malle: A European Outsider in the American Mainstream', in Wendy Everett (ed.) *European Identity in Cinema* (Bristol: Intellect): 30–4.

Johnstone, Sheila (1990) 'The History Man', *The Independent* 17 August: 12.

Kael, Pauline (1975) *Deeper into the Movies: The Essential Kael Collection: from '69 to '72* (London: Marion Boyars).

McCabe, Colin (1974) 'Realism and the Cinema: Notes on some Brechtian Theses', *Screen* 15.2: 7–26.

Malle, Louis (1974) *Audio Tape Interviews from the National Film Theatre London* (London: BFI).

Malle, Louis (1974b) 'Le cinéma français et le star-system', *Le Film Français* 8 February: 4–6.

Malle, Louis (1978) *Louis Malle par Louis Malle* (Paris: Editions de l'Athanor).

Malle, Louis (1979) 'Creating a Reality that Doesn't Exist: An Interview with Louis Malle', *Literature/Film Quarterly* 7.2: 86–98.

Malle, Louis (1988) 'Louis Malle' in C. Devarrieux and M.-C. De Navacelle (eds), *Cinéma du réel* (Paris: Autrément): 22–31.

Malle, Louis (1999) 'Louis Malle on *Au revoir les enfants*', *Projections* 9: 33–50.

Malle, Louis and Jean-Louis Ezine (1986) 'Quand vous étiez cinéaste ...' *Le Nouvel Observateur* 14 March.

Malle, Louis and Philip French (1993) *Malle on Malle* (London: Faber & Faber).

Marsolais, Gilles (1974) *Cinéma Direct* (Paris: Seghers).

Prédal, René (1989) *Louis Malle* (Paris: Edilig).

Queneau, Raymond (1959) *Zazie dans le métro* (Paris: Gallimard).

Roud, Richard (1989) 'Malle x 4' *Sight and Sound* (spring): 125–7.

Virmaux, Alain, and Odette Virmaux (1976) *Les Surréalistes et le cinéma* (Paris: Seghers).

Yates, Robert (1994) 'Louis the 42nd', *Guardian* 17 Dec.: 24.

Yule, Andrew (1988) *David Puttnam: The Story So Far* (London: Sphere).

3

Active pessimism and the politics of the 1950s

Readers may well have extrapolated from Malle's contribution to the events of May '68 and his films of the 1970s and 1980s that the director, despite his social origins, was broadly speaking from the left-wing of the political spectrum. In fact, Malle is a far more politically fluid film-maker than his later work implies. As Malle was to himself admit, he once held complex cultural affinities with the radical right-wing, although these were in themselves subtle and ambiguous connections (1978: 71–2). In the first part of this chapter I will discuss *Ascenseur pour l'échafaud*, *Les Amants* and *Le Feu follet* in the light of this admission.

The chapter also offers an opportunity to analyse Malle's political journey from the cultural right-wing to the libertarian left, to explain how *Le Souffle au cœur* (1971) marked a radical break with the 1950s by speaking of that era through a comic mode. In this context, the subject of the representation of women in Mallean film is an important point of comparison. On the one hand, the politics of Mallean film evolved over time to a unique version of post-May '68 libertarianism. Conversely, the conservative portrayal of women in his cinema remained relatively stable throughout the oeuvre.

Fascism and the politics of active pessimism

Malle's collaboration with royalist novelist Roger Nimier on the *film noir*, *Ascenseur pour l'échafaud* (1957) was a commercial and critical triumph. However, it also provoked a scathing critique by Raymond

Borde. Writing for the periodical *Les Temps modernes*, Borde was especially severe towards Malle and the political slant that he identified in his film. Very publicly, Borde accused Malle of having produced a politically repugnant work. He concluded his three-page review with the following commentary: 'Un petit dur à la mode, un parachutiste de trente-cinq ans, un capitaliste néo-nazi, voilà les trois repères du rêve intérieur de Louis Malle. A tous les sens du mot, *Ascenseur pour l'échafaud* est un film fasciste' (1958: 1910).[1] Prior to this final twist of the rhetorical knife, Borde presented a detailed critique of why he felt the film evoked these 'phantasmes chers au petits gens de droite' ('fantasies dear to small-time right-wing people'). He argued that Malle's film was obsessed with signs of wealth, Mercedes cars and luxurious office blocks. Similarly, Borde felt that his presentation of a German businessman pandered to a contemporary right-wing fantasy for strong Germans who had survived the Second World War and who were now prospering in the new Europe of the Treaty of Rome and the Common Market. Coincidentally, a similar figure had been offered by Curt Jürgens in Roger Vadim's *Et Dieu créa la femme* (1956). Even more perturbing than Malle's German was the portrayal of the paratrooper anti-hero, Julien Tavernier (Maurice Ronet). Tavernier was a veteran of the Indochina and Algerian campaigns who had left the frontline to serve as a personal assistant to a powerful company chairman. Borde distrusted the positive image Malle and his scriptwriter Nimier had established of a character who was essentially an assassin. A third character from the film, the youth who steels Tavernier's car and revolver, was a similar thug, just fifteen years younger but without the Saint-Cyr military academy training.

Borde used the politically loaded term fascist far too quickly in this review. *Ascenseur pour l'échafaud* is not an overtly political picture. Nonetheless, Borde's attack cannot be entirely dismissed as dated polemic. As several film scholars have more recently highlighted, the wars of decolonisation in Indochina and Algeria did mark much of Malle's early work (Nicholls: 1996). The central protagonists from both *Ascenseur pour l'échafaud* and later *Le Feu follet* are veterans of these conflicts. As David Nicholls has described, in some ways

1 'A fashionable little tough guy, a 35-year-old paratrooper, a Neo-Nazi capitalist, make up the three reference points of Louis Malle's inner dream. In every sense of the word, *Ascenseur pour l'échafaud* is a fascist film.'

continuing the original critique offered by Raymond Borde in the original *Les Temps modernes* review, Tavernier 'retains a kind of fascistic purity, a battered Parsifal who has passed through the rite of passage of the colonial wars, but whose ultimate fate is humiliation not glory' (1996: 278). Anticipating Nicholl's judgement other scholars have also noted that actors like Maurice Ronet were gradually being typecast in Malle's films as 'Jeune homme de droite' ('Young right-wing men') (Daniel 1972: 402; see also De Comès and Marmin 1985: 30–1). Thus, Malle's first male lead actor subtly perpetuated militarist myths that surrounded the conflicts in Indochina and Algeria. Notably, the characters of Tavernier (*Ascenseur*) and Alain (*Le Feu follet*) are shown to be attractive, fascinating masculine anti-heroes who have returned from the frontline to a nation that was not willing to support their war effort or to assist in their reintegration into society. To that extent Malle, Nimier and Ronet were playing with popular right-wing myths that were common at that time. Moreover, in bringing them to the cinema screens they were perpetuating the fantasy, with Ronet personifying the figure of the disgusted but heroic war veteran lost in a cruel world.

Despite the interpretative connections to be made between Malle and the after-shocks of decolonisation, I think Nicholls is too swift to see this element of the films as reflecting the core political values of Malle's work at the end of the Fourth and beginning of the Fifth Republic. More importantly, several of his early films shared deeper cultural sensibilities with the fictional universe created by the extreme right-leaning novelists such as Roger Nimier, Antoine Blondin, Jacques Chardonne or Paul Morand. As René Prédal has explained, on the level of emotional–psychological interest Malle's filmic universe in this period often chimed with his first scriptwriter Roger Nimier's better-known outlook. Prédal carefully analyses the connections:

> Or les œuvres suivantes de Malle montrerait qu'existe en réalité une véritable symbiose entre les deux regards [Malle and Nimier] sur la société de l'époque. Le suicide, le dégoût ou l'indifférence des héros de Nimier trouveront leurs répandants du côté des personnages du *Feu Follet*, de *Vie privée*, voire même du *Voleur* ou de *William Wilson* malgré la force des textes originaux dont ils sont tirés. Les idées de mort, d'autodestruction amère de protagonistes fatigués, perdus dans un monde de vieux sans idéaux où les nouvelles générations ne savent pas à quelles valeurs se raccrocher, circulent entre littéraire et cinéma

jusqu'à ce que Malle dédie à Nimier le scénario du *Souffle au cœur*. (1989: 13)[2]

Rightly, Prédal underlines the emotional themes that Malle and Nimier explored in the 1950s and into the mid-1960s. The keywords are: suicide, disgust, indifference, death, decadence, loss and failure. In fact, the same thematic territory was once briefly highlighted by Malle as a key element in his loosely defined political philosophy. Writing in his co-authored memoirs (1978), Malle declared his complicated cultural–political feelings:

> Mais j'ai une conviction intime: je ne serai jamais pour l'ordre établi. Malraux a écrit 'Tout l'homme actif et pessimiste à la fois est ou deviendra fasciste, sauf s'il a une fidèlité derrière lui'. Je suis actif, et pessimiste, mais je sais aussi à quoi je suis fidèle: c'est ce matin de janvier 1944 où j'ai vu le jeune garçon juif qui était dans ma classe se lever à l'entrée de gestapistes, et nous serrer la main l'un après l'autre, en nous regardant dans les yeux. (Malle, with Mallecot 1978: 71–2)[3]

Malle's personal and artistic fidelity to 'January 1944' and the events he would later film as *Au revoir les enfants* are indisputable (see Chapter 5 for my discussion of this film and its wider implications for understanding Malle's work). In the context of our current discussion the earlier part of the statement is of greater importance. It shows that Malle accepted that he was drawn to a psychological position close to André Malraux's definition of fascism – a position that led to his attraction to filmic equivalents to the fiction of writers like Nimier or

2 'Now, Malle's next works show that in fact a real symbiosis exists between the two men's [Malle and Nimier] perspectives on contemporary society. The suicide, the disgust, or the indifference of Nimier's heroes are found spread throughout the protagonists of *Feu Follet*, *Vie privée*, even in *Voleur* or *William Wilson*, despite the power of the original sources from which they were adapted. The ideas of death, the bitter self-destruction of exhausted characters lost in an old world without ideals, where the new generation does not know which values to follow, move between literature and cinema until Malle dedicated the screen play of *Souffle au cœur* to Nimier.'

3 'But I have an intimate conviction: I will never be in favour of the established order of things. Malraux has written: "Every man who is at once active and pessimistic is, or will be, fascist, except if he has a fidelity to support him." I am active, and pessimistic, but I also know what I am loyal to: it is to that morning in January 1944 when I saw the young Jewish boy who was in my class stand up when the Gestapo entered the room, and shake our hands, one after the other of us, while looking us in the eyes.'

indeed the fascist novelist Pierre Drieu La Rochelle, whose work he would adapt in his fifth film, *Le Feu follet*.

A brief résumé of the basic plots of Malle's *Les Amants*, *Vie privée* or *Le Feu follet* confirm Malle's propensity for active pessimism. All three of the aforementioned films are set among the bored, *mondaine* and mundane lives of the social elite. Both *Vie privée* and *Le Feu follet* end with violent and pointless deaths. Each of the films suggest that the micro-worlds that they depict have lost their capacity to survive but continue to glorify the aristocratic manners of yesteryear, without even much belief in them anymore. The central protagonists – played by Jeanne Moreau, Brigitte Bardot and Maurice Ronet respectively, share a kind of world weariness which constrains their every move. There are no overtly expressed political views here, just an over-powering sense of discontentment with the world and a pessimism that clearly does not originate on the socialist left wing and so by implication drifts towards a quirky, individualistic, form of right-wing anxiety about the modern world.

Le Feu follet is the most powerful demonstration of active pessimism in Mallean film. Neither the original novel nor the film version of *Le Feu follet* are overtly political. Inspired by the life and death of Drieu la Rochelle's friend, Jacques Rigaut, it is the story of Alain Leroy (Ronet) and his psychological descent to the point of suicide. The novel is constructed through Alain's last days of attempting to recover from opium addiction, adapted in the film to alcoholism. Seeking some kind of meaning beyond his addiction, or his superficial high-society living, Alain visits several old friends. Neither male nor female relationships prove sufficient to prevent Leroy's fatal destiny. The film and the novel conclude with Alain's suicide. Leroy takes his own life with a single shot to the heart, fired from a Luger pistol, a prop that is rumoured to have been Malle's own weapon. The central protagonist can neither tolerate his own life nor that of his contemporaries. Everything is either betrayal or com-promise. Alain's only honest escape from his psychological crisis is his sudden but predictable death.

The narrative I summarise, and that Malle executed on film, offers a radical subtext. Alain has literally nothing to live for and this is a damning, latently political, critique of contemporary society. The viewer is posed the question: why will Alain take his life? One of the answers that Malle–Drieu evoke is because he is decadent and cannot live with either his own or society's mediocrity. Here, Malle's updating of the original novel to the 1960s is central. Had the piece remained historical then the implied criticism would have been attenuated. However, Malle's updating, which includes brief references to the defeat in Algeria, sharpens the message. Alain cannot survive because he and France are decadent. To paraphrase the implication, society must change for there to be stronger men than Alain Leroy. This is the ambivalent political element of the otherwise neo-romantic sensibility displayed in *Le Feu follet*.

Reread in the light of *Le Feu follet*, Malle's second film *Les Amants* can be seen to sketch out a complementary moral. Let us survey the main protagonists from that film and the cultural values that Malle implicitly ascribes to them. First, there is Jeanne's lover, Raoul Florès. He is a Spanish aristocrat and polo champion, an outsider and a decadent Parisian figure who does not hold the heroine's attention, let alone shape her inner life. Second, there is Jeanne's husband, M. Henri Tournier. Memorably played by Alain Cuny, he is shown to be too trapped in the commercial world of the Dijonnais press to capture his wife's heart. It seems that the crude world of finance has ruined him. Finally, there is Jeanne's second, temporarily successful, lover. This is the young student, Bernard Dubois-Lambert (Jean-Luc Bory). Ultimately, it is this character who opens up vistas of passion for Jeanne, and who at the end of the film tentatively leads her towards a different life, apart from Raoul and Henri. Let us look more closely at this positively valorised lover. He is neither foreign nor tainted by cheap money or provincial commerce but is instead a student of archaeology. Later, we learn that he has rejected the decadent Parisian lifestyle of his aristocratic but decadent relatives to study the very foundations of civilisation itself. Thus, when he first encounters Jeanne's broken-down car on the highway he is carrying a specimen of rock to show to his worthy old professor. Named Dubois-Lambert, he is also from the right social class but, moreover, he is shown by Malle to be willing to break away from its decaying sterility.

The meaning of the love triangle in *Les Amants* is implicit, but very real. I think that Malle's film implies that for the young wife Jeanne to find herself truly, she needs to forge a relationship with a Frenchman of the new generation, with a man who is respectful of the past and dismissive of the decadence of the present. Jeanne's husband and lover have failed her. But in the fantasy played out in *Les Amants* her sterile family life will be replaced with the young archaeologist Bernard Dubois-Lambert. Here, the character of Bernard in *Les Amants* offers the inverse stereotype of Alain from *Le Feu follet*. Bernard is psychologically grounded and a sexually virile individual. Alain is an addict, sterile and decadent, a failed man in every sense of the word. Bernard and Alain are opposite poles of the same right-wing fantasy of masculinity. One man represents pure athleticism, the other, the constant temptation of decadence. The one character requiring its twin to gain legitimacy and lend the filmic discourse authority and coherence.

To repeat, Malle's films of the 1950s converged with the world of the extreme right-wing literary tradition, often loosely defined as 'the Hussard' movement, a term coined by the critic Bernard Frank (1952) and that also evokes Nimier's novel *Le Hussard bleu* (1950). The ideological correspondence at play was more a matter of tone and subtle narrative implication than of any programmatic or didactic political commitment. Malle's attraction to pessimism and despair was the central point where his work intersected with similar psychological and cultural dispositions held on the literary right wing. There is a mutual disgust with post-war bourgeois society, a common loathing of the modern world, and a fear of the ever-present threat of decadence. In holding these emotional and poetic perspectives, sometimes the young Malle fell into a cultural discourse of the right.

Returning to the *fascisant* themes of that era in 1988, Malle explained his view at that time but tellingly did not apologise for them. Speaking of Nimier, he asserted:

> En fait, beaucoup de gens détestaient Nimier. Je le savais mais en même temps je l'admirais personellement beaucoup et il était de toute manière reconnu comme un des grands talents de sa génération. Bien sûr, il a ensuite pris des positions franchement pro-OAS sur l'Algérie et j'ai alors cessé de le voir pendant près de deux ans: nous avions vraiment des convictions politiques trop opposés. C'est un peu la même chose qui s'est produite quand j'ai adapté *Le Feu follet*: toute idéologie de Drieu la Rochelle m'a été collée sur le dos! ... Alors qu'en fait il ne s'agissait que d'accords de sensibilités. Ce qui m'avait intéressé dans le livre de Drieu la Rochelle était la question du suicide de son ami (qui n'était pas du tout fasciste) et nullement le destin politique de l'auteur. (cited in Prédal: 14)[4]

4 'In fact, many people hated Nimier. I knew that but at the same time, personally, I admired him greatly. Anyway, he was recognised as one of the major talents of

In hindsight Malle's distinction between extreme right-wing 'politics' and extreme-right-wing 'sensibility' is more problematic than the director ever publicly acknowledged. There is a fine line between being fascinated by a milieu's cultural or social values and supporting its more general ideology. As I have shown in my readings of *Le Feu follet* and *Les Amants* Malle's cinema often works along the fine edge of this line. Those films allowed viewers to glimpse the world of right-wing sensibilities without fully articulating the wider political implications. Readers should also consider that in the context of the 1950s and 1960s cultural politics was all that was really left for the inheritors of the ultra-royalist *Action française* (Weber 1962: 520). To share extreme-right-wing, 'Hussard', sensibilities was however unintentionally also to engage in that group's only relatively successful public endeavour.

Provocatively, an element of the political ambiguities that surround Malle's early work are captured in his mid-1960s film, *Le Voleur*. As if acknowledging his own contradictory past, Malle introduces a discussion between two anarchists who are shown observing an extreme nationalist, anti-Semitic, political rally of around the time of the Dreyfus affair. The less important figure, Cannonier, explains how he would destroy them all. He declares: 'If I had some dynamite ... I would put it in the middle of that table'. The central protagonist Randal, who might well stand for Malle, replies: 'I would stop you ... because of a lady who is there ... whom I care about' (Malle and Boulanger 1967: 30). It is plausible to suggest that Malle's attitude to the extreme right-wing was repeatedly closer to Randal's individualistic charity than to Cannonier's bolder but less subtle antifascism.

---

his generation. Of course, regarding Algeria he followed political positions that were frankly in favour of the OAS and at that time I stopped seeing him for nearly two years. We really did have too divergent political convictions. It's a little bit the same thing that happened when I adapted *Le Feu follet*: Drieu's ideology was pinned on me ... In fact it was only a matter of agreement of sensibilities. What had interested me in Drieu la Rochelle's book was the question of the suicide of his friend (who wasn't at all a fascist) and not in the least the political destiny of its author.'

Louis Malle and the 'Hussards'

It is important to present some further contextual material to support
the interpretation of the 1950s films I have just developed. This more
biographical and historical exploration of social and political contacts
that Malle developed in the 1950s precedes the next section of the
book where I explore how Malle's representation of women often
implicitly also supports my contention on the politics of his 1950s
films.

During and after the making of *Ascenseur pour l'échafaud* Malle
became known as a playboy celebrity, living from the success of the
Cousteau collaboration, *Le Monde du silence*, and the reputation of the
Béghin family. Film festivals, champagne and the accoutrements of
the high life were Malle's for the taking and the director enjoyed
much that this world had to offer. In *Ascenseur pour l'échafaud*
Tavernier drove his Mercedes convertible, while in reality Malle
owned a Jaguar, and scriptwriter Nimier was obsessed with his Aston
Martin. New social friends also marked Malle out as being part of the
social world Raymond Borde had identified in his review of *Ascenseur
pour l'échafaud*. Beside Cousteau and the 'naval set' whom he had met
when making *Le Monde du silence*, Malle spent time with his then
partner Jeanne Moreau, as well as Nimier, Ronet, the classical actor
Alain Cuny and the *haute-bourgeoise* novelist, Louise de Vilmorin. As
Malle later acknowledged in those days he 'was living by night',
quickly exchanging scriptwriting sessions with Nimier or de Vilmorin
for parties and the seductive combination of pretty people, success,
wealth and alcohol (Malle and French 1993: 43). Arguably, without
pursuing any strict sociological analysis to support the case, the
novelist Louise de Vilmorin was at the centre of a dominant social set
of which Malle was a welcome part. A close friend of Nimier, de
Vilmorin's house parties at 'Verrières' were legendary. Her 'club de
Verrières', or the 'Verrières set', included Malle, his lover Moreau, his
scriptwriter Nimier, as well as François Truffaut, Françoise Sagan
(author of the hit novel *Bonjour tristesse* (1954) later filmed by Otto
Preminger) and many other personalities of the 1950s (see Bothorel
1993: 253). Nimier was an obsessive correspondent with de Vilmorin,
and fell in love with her.

Malle's cultural milieu did have significant right-wing political
overtones. Among the actors, writers and film-makers that were part

of his circle there were influential figures who were closer to the far-right-wing literary scene than perhaps Malle would have wished to later acknowledge. First and foremost, there is of course Roger Nimier. He was at the heart of the 'Hussard' literary movement that broadly speaking continued the tradition of the royalist *Action française* movement into the 1950s (Hewitt 1996; Dambre 1989). The author of some five novels, Nimier's famous *Le Hussard bleu* (1950) attacked both Gaullist and Communist currents of the resistance that were perceived to have profited from the liberation. It is a bitter satire on the French conduct of war during the German campaign of 1944–5. Similarly, by the mid-1950s Nimier was also active in his attempts to rehabilitate the work of extreme-right-wing writers who had been active in the inter-war years but who had subsequently been compromised by their activities under the Vichy regime (Jackson 2002: 609; Hewitt 1996: 75–104). Among the many figures whom he supported via his editorship at the Gallimard publishing house were Pierre Drieu la Rochelle, Jacques Chardonne, Paul Morand, and most importantly, the extreme anti-Semite, Louis-Ferdinand Céline.

Nimier's cultural–political plans sometimes included a role for Malle. For example, Nimier had introduced Malle to the notorious Céline, spending time together at the writer's home, Meudon (Malle and Dambre 1989: 14). Nimier and Céline had even thought of encouraging Malle to produce and direct a film of the later's famous novel, *Voyage au bout de la nuit*. Writing to Céline on 22 November 1960, Nimier explained: 'J'attends que mon ami Louis Malle soit rentré à Paris pour lui proposer le "Voyage au bout de la nuit". L'avantage serait double: a) C'est un excellent metteur en scène. b) Il a une société de production qui a fait jusqu'ici de très bonnes affaires' (Nimier in Fouché ed. 1991: 549).[5] Céline's reply was acidic and pessimistic in equal measure: 'A parier encore que ce Prince du cinéma est parti dans la Lune chercher des idées, qu'il reviendra dans dix ans' (Céline in Fouché ed. 1991: 549).[6] When Malle published a

---

5 'I am waiting until my friend Louis Malle has returned to Paris to propose to him *Voyage au bout de la nuit*. The advantage will be twofold: (a) He is an excellent director. (b) he has a production company that has until now done very good business.'

6 'We must be prepared to bet that the prince of cinema leaves for the moon in search of ideas and he only then returns to earth in ten years' time.'

list of incomplete film projects in the late 1970s he made no reference to this project and so perhaps it was never discussed in detail (Malle 1978: 73–6). As we know this film was never realised and later Céline spoke to another director, Claude Autant-Lara, inviting him to bring the novel to the screen (Céline in Fouché ed. 1991: 582). Other right-wing literary personalities were more impressed with *Ascenseur pour l'échafaud* than Céline implied in his correspondence with Nimier. The young novelist received praise for the film from the aristocratic writer, Jacques Chardonne. Chardonne had been another sympathetic supporter of the Vichy regime, considering it the best hope for the ruralist, romantic vision of France that he advocated in his fiction (Jackson 2003: 205–6). His anticipation for the Nimier–Malle–Ronet picture was expressed in a letter to the scriptwriter. Herein, he exuded support for the film: 'J'irai bientôt voir cet *Ascenseur*. Les bruits sont excitants. Ils promettent énormément' (Chardonne and Nimier 1984: 219).[7] However, Nimier's reply displayed less enthusiasm for the finished work, describing it as incoherent, combining some idiotic scenes with others that were of a better quality. Continuing the modest tone of the letter he thanked Chardonne for a line he had borrowed for the script (Chardonne and Nimier 1984: 220). The phrase he referred to was the cynical comment on contemporary history made by the German business-man who boasts to his young French companion about the post-war Franco-German truce, 'After all, we are all travelling salesman now'.

In addition to his friendship with Nimier and the contacts that came with it, Malle was also a one-time social companion of the famous *bon viveur* and sports journalist for *L'Equipe*, Antoine Blondin. Blondin, another of the so-called 'Hussard' novelists, also wrote articles for the marginal neo-fascist weekly paper *Rivarol*. Like Nimier, his fiction disrupted comfortable images of a '*France résistante*'. The intimacy of the Malle–Blondin–Nimier friendship is hinted at in a published account of their final conversation, conducted on the morning before Nimier's infamous death in a road accident. Blondin recalled: 'Le matin de l'accident, nous bavardions avec Louis Malle. Ce dernier, et par ailleurs ce benjamin, baignait dans la mélancolie d'avoir bientôt trente ans; – Comme je vous comprends,

---

7 'I am going to see *Ascenseur* soon. The rumours are exciting. They are enormously promising.'

lui dit Roger, il vous faut encore attendre vingt ans d'en avoir cinquante. Nous avons de l'avance sur vous' (cited in Nimier and Chardonne 1984: 305).[8] For what it is worth, one might also add here that Malle and Blondin covered the same Tour de France cycle race in 1962, one as a print journalist for *l'Equipe* magazine, the other in preparation for the short film, *Vive le Tour* (shot 1962, produced 1965). Blondin even joked in one of his articles about the presence of the maker of *Le Monde du silence* being now on dry land to film that year's Tour ([1963] 1991: 1322). Coincidentally, Blondin would also later exchange his sportswriter's pen for that of the film critic to praise the completed film, *Le Feu follet* (Blondin cited Chapier 1964: 170–2). In fact, Malle had initially hoped that their mutual friend Roger Nimier would adapt the scenario from the original Drieu la Rochelle novel (Malle and Dambre 1989: 16).

Another figure from a similar political milieu was the star of both *Ascenseur pour l'échafaud* and *Le Feu follet*, actor Maurice Ronet. A friend of Malle and Blondin, Ronet gravitated to the extreme right wing of cultural politics. The film historians Beylie and d'Hugues have described his politics: 'Comme plusieurs amis de sa génération, il ne songeait nullement à dissimuler une orientation personnelle, qui, au-delà du désenchantement et en réaction, le portait de plus en plus vers les écrivains de droite comme Drieu la Rochelle, Brasillach ou Céline' (1999: 275; for comparable discussion of Ronet see also de Comès and Marmin 1985: 30–1).[9] Ronet was also to work on the Antoine Blondin scripted film *Le Dernier Saut* (1969 directed by Edmund Luntz) and shortly before his death, in 1983, on an unfinished version of Céline's *Semmelweis*.

While working with Cousteau on *Le Monde du silence*, Malle met the marine director's brother, the hard right-wing journalist Pierre Antoine Cousteau (a sometime editor of, again, *Rivarol*) and, through this connection, also the disgraced anti-Semitic novelist and film

8 'The morning of the accident we were chatting with Louis Malle. The aforementioned youngster was swimming in melancholy about soon being 30 years old; Roger told him he understood this entirely, for he would have to wait another twenty years before reaching fifty. We were some way in advance of him.'

9 'Like several friends of his generation, he never dreamed of hiding his personal views, which, beyond disenchantment and reaction, took him nearer and nearer to right-wing writers like Drieu la Rochelle, Brasillach or Céline.'

critic, Lucien Rebatet (Malle 1978: 41). In addition to his editorship of
Rivarol, Pierre Antoine Cousteau continued to publish extreme-right-
wing pamphlets and books throughout much of the 1950s. He was
frank about his past and present political opinions. For example,
Julian Jackson cites one memorable passage from P. A. Cousteau's
writing that offers a flavour of his dogmatic approach. P. A. Cousteau
wrote: 'if I adopted, in 1941, an attitude of collaboration, it was not to
limit the damage ... or play some kind of double game. It was because
I wanted a German victory ... because it represented ... the last chance
of the white man, while the democracies represented the end of the
white man' (cited in Jackson 2002: 610). Just shortly after these
remarks were expressed the racist journalist fell seriously ill. For
whatever motivations, Malle offered a blood transfusion to try to save
his life (Violet 1993: 150). The two men shared the same blood group,
zero negative, so it was hoped the transfusion would be a success. It
failed and Pierre Antoine Cousteau was no longer able to continue his
interventions in the political debates of the late 1950s. Jacques
Cousteau and indeed also Malle, continued their ever popular film
careers. Intriguingly, Jacques Cousteau's own politics have recently
been the subject of historical controversy and revision. Jacques
Cousteau is described in the Malle–French interviews as being a
member of the resistance (1993: 101). However, Bernard Violet's
recent biography explains that the grounds for this claim are more
limited than one might expect. Despite his involvement in espionage,
in 1943 Cousteau had also participated in a documentary-film festival
supported by the Vichy regime (1993: 72). His first short underwater
films had been a success of the Vichy years, even drawing positive
reviews from the anti-Semitic novelist Lucien Rebatet writing for the
collaborationist literary journal, *Je Suis Partout* (see Violet 1993: 73–4;
and see also Henley 1999: 17).

   Bernard Violet suggests that Malle's blood transfusion to save
Pierre Antoine Cousteau was an elegant gesture, a sign of Malle's
support for a dying man (1993: 150). The episode – which is of some
biographical interest – is ignored in the Philip French–Louis Malle
interview (1993) and is likewise neither discussed in Billard's treatment (2003) nor as part of the Malle and Marc Dambre interview on
Roger Nimier (1989). The impression left in the Malle–French
interviews was that many of the friendships and political encounters
of the era were relatively short-lived and inconsequential. French

asked Malle about Nimier's politics, saying: 'he was a writer of the political right, wasn't he?'. Malle replied: 'Yes, but that became more apparent later on, especially at the time of the Algerian war, when intellectuals had to take sides' (1993: 11). Malle's assessment here is a little disingenuous. Nimier had never concealed his political affiliations or preferences and any reading of his fiction shows that he had 'taken sides' long before the war in Algeria had developed. Notwithstanding Malle's later gloss on the 1950s it is evident from historical analysis of the era that extreme-right-wing intellectuals and fellow-travellers like Nimier, Blondin and Ronet enjoyed Malle's company. They also sometimes sought to recuperate him to their cultural agenda, *qua* the unsuccessful Céline film project. Furthermore, irrespective of any differences that emerged between them over the question of war in Algeria, by 1962 Malle had thought of renewing professional contacts with Nimier to work on the script of his film of the Drieu la Rochelle inspired, *Le Feu follet*.

How is the film historian to understand the types of relationship that I have been presenting? Let us be clear: the borders between literary and cinematic activity and political commitment do not offer simple black and white answers. Once more Malle throws us into the realm of ambiguity. On the one hand, friendships, common cultural interests and preferences are perhaps not the most accurate guides to straightforward definitions of ideological positions. On the other hand, in subtle ways Malle's social connections and film projects overlapped and mirrored each other. Malle's work did slide into a wider tradition of right-wing literary anarchism and romantic reaction. Sometimes, the friendships and cultural links were overt, as in the case of planning to invite Nimier to script *Le Feu follet*. Sometimes, they were less pronounced, if present at all as in a project like *Vie privée* or *Zazie dans le métro* (a film which concludes with a chaotic anti-fascist battle). Like Malle's relationship with the New Wave, discussed in Chapter 1 of this book, we should not look for certainties but rather locate Malle as a figure who moved in and out of a loosely defined political–literary milieu. Perhaps it is only in political science textbooks, or debating chambers, that political ideologies are one dimensional and clear cut. In life, in Malle's life at least, they are more fluid, unsystematic, and ever-shifting. One can be on the right wing, share some psychological and emotional perspectives with figures like a Nimier or a Blondin, without participating in their wider journalistic activities. One could break with Nimier over the Algerian war but still consider working with him afterwards. One could remain loyal to the victims of the Holocaust while also attempting to save the life of a fatally ill former collaborator. Malle's life and work in the 1950s are made up of exactly these types of contradiction.

Cultural context offers more clarity. In hindsight, Malle was just one director in a wider undefined network of right-leaning cultural activists at work in the cinema in the late 1950s. To repeat, the figure of Nimier is the predominant personality, the key interface between Malle, the film industry and the right wing. Along with working with Malle, he also collaborated with Michelangelo Antonioni and Jacques Becker (d'Hugues 1995). Likewise, in 1960, Jean Valère brought Nimier's novel, *Histoire d'un amour* to the screen as *Les Grandes Personnes*. It again starred Maurice Ronet. It is this type of recurrence that gives me confidence that, although shadowy in form, a loose right-wing cultural–filmic rearguard action was being fought.

This unplanned project that almost dared not speak its own name was nevertheless responsible for a significant quantity of cultural products. For example, beyond Malle, there are also unclassifiable reactionary figures like Paul Gégauff, the friend and scriptwriter to Claude Chabrol (de Baecque 1997: 88–91). His preference was for grotesque shows of right-wing provocation, once storming into a cinema showing of the British war film *Went the Day Well* dressed in the garb of a Nazi officer (de Baecque 1997: 88). Notoriously, working with Claude Chabrol in *Les Cousins* (1958) he reprised the scene, showing a student party that culminates in a similar fascist fantasy. Other young 'Hussards' found similar cinematic success. One can quickly recall the Henri Verneuil adaptation of Antoine Blondin's novel *Un singe en hiver* (1962). A third 'Hussard' novelist, Jacques Laurent was also a prolific source for contemporary film-makers, offering source material, or scripts for projects. His better-known works are *Lola Montès* (1955 directed by Max Ophuls) and *Caroline Chérie* (1957).

The impact of Marcel Aymé was equally important. The best-known example of his influence was his script for the occupation-set satire, *Traversée de Paris* (1958 directed by Autant-Lara). In addition, Aymé's fiction was also brought to the screen in several other films, including: *La Belle Image* (1951, directed by Claude Heymann); *Passe-*

Muraille (1951, directed by Jean Broyer); *Papa, Mama et la Bonne Fois* (1954, directed by Jean-Paul Le Chanois); *Le Chemin des écoliers* (1962, directed by Michel Boisrond) and *La Jument Verte* (1959 again directed by Claude Autant-Lara). The Aymé–Autant–Lara partnership is especially illustrative of the as yet undefined current in French film that I am piecing together. Both men were self-styled *anarchistes de droites* and, most controversially, Autant-Lara finished his career as a Front National member of the European Parliament, Strasbourg.

Placed in this wider historical context, the cultural pessimism displayed by Malle can be situated in a network of 1950s right-wing cultural activities. Interestingly, the political affiliations of figures like Nimier, Gégauff, Malle, Chabrol, Autant-Lara or Aymé cut across traditional aesthetic categories like 'New Wave' or 'traditional film-making', appearing in different contexts and on different occasions. The young Malle was just one member of a flexible and shifting group of directors, actors, scriptwriters and novelists who wore their political colours lightly but were nonetheless commonly engaged in producing a cinema shaped by right-wing political sensibilities.

Reactionary politics and the representation of women

If a romantic, reactionary vision of active pessimism underscored late 1950s Mallean cinema, it is also important to recall that Malle's representation of women in these films is shaped by a comparable outlook. As Geneviève Sellier suggests in her groundbreaking work, women frequently form decorative, objectified elements in Malle's narratives ((with Vincendeau) 1998; 2001). The presentation of Brigitte Bardot in *Vie privée* is shaped by a masculinist outlook. Sellier explains that while Malle's film had intended to be a study of the star phenomenon, a quasi-biographical picture that dissected the Bardot myth, the end result of *Vie privée* was very different. In its place, there is a depiction that first objectifies the star and then presents her through a series of stereotypes, all of which rely on sexist assumptions. Here, Jill (Bardot) is an intellectually weak woman associated with mass culture. Her only area of independence is that of sexual choice. Sellier explains: for Jill 'femininity is associated with sexuality as its principal identity, while male characters in the film have a social and professional identity' (2001: 132). Echoing this view, Ginette

Vincendeau adds: 'films [Malle's and Godard's *Le Mépris*] reduce her [Bardot's] character to female sexuality and, as such, to the opposite of creativity' (2000: 105). These arguments are persuasive, and they are all the more so when read alongside Malle's more general politico-cultural disposition that I have outlined above. A sense of conser-vatism in the portrayal of women runs in parallel to the political discourses I have noted.

Neither *Les Amants* nor *Vie privée* represent Malle's most sexist work. That status is reserved for the Edgar Alan Poe adaptation, *William Wilson* (1967). Once more starring Bardot, the film includes several scenes of gratuitous male sexual violence against women. Such scenes point to a misogynist streak in Mallean film that is less subtle and complex than even the relationships presented in *Les Amants* or *Vie privée*. In Malle's defence one should note that he has looked back on *William Wilson* with some regret, telling Philip French, 'I was in a strange mood: dark, very dark, suicidal' (1993: 66). Nonetheless, Malle and Philip French do not discuss how this mood came to be played out as visual rhetoric of woman-hating sado-masochism in *William Wilson*. Instead, the men continue to discuss Malle's memory of his childhood and how its shadow was cast over the scenes from the same film that are set in a boys' boarding school and so anticipate *Au revoir les enfants*.

As Malle gradually evolved into the 1960s radical libertarian, his cinematic portrayals of women and sexuality failed to adjust to a more self-conscious position. Writing in *Film Quarterly* in 1974 Todd Gitlin identifies a deeply problematic passage from the documentary *L'Inde fantôme*. He explains:

he takes us to what he calls the 'ideal society of villagers'. They have no wars, no laws, no weapons. The eight hundred of them have resisted missionaries, the English, tourists – and film-makers. They have, Malle says, 'sexual freedom.' The women are sexually 'initiated' by 'experienced' men at the age of thirteen – Malle does not say how the men are 'initiated.' Women are apparently common property, and are given to kissing the feet of men – but not vice versa. Malle does not comment on this iniquity in what he calls a 'perfect society': he merely nostalgically observes that the villagers will be soon evicted, as their land has been taken for turpentine cultivation. Later on, he interviews a Western-trained economist and refers to her, condescendingly, as 'this very pretty young woman'. With such images of the 'ideal society'

... it is fair to say that Malle should not allow himself to indulge his attitudes. (60)[10]

So, Malle's 1950s masculinist outlook was gradually replaced with a 1970s variant on the discourse of sexual liberation, a discourse that also worked to the advantage of men and to the continued objectification of women. Mallean fiction in this period is replete with male fantasies: the young boy successfully making love with his attractive mother (*Le Souffle au cœur*); and the young girl becoming the subject of adult male fascination (Violet in *Pretty Baby*). In short, Mallean film confirms Laura Mulvey's now classic thesis on the representation of women in narrative cinema (1975). Furthermore, it also extended the traditional male perspective of the objectifying gaze from fiction into the field of documentary. As noted above, this was already a disturbing aspect of the *Inde fantôme* series. However, lest we should imagine that Malle was exclusively driven by a neo-colonial drive, the westerner's exotic–erotic visual domination of Indian women, let us next turn to an example taken from his documentary work in the United States.

Malle's *God's Country* is a charming and powerful documentary on the mid-west in the early 1980s. One symbolically important scene assists my discussion in that it neatly encapsulates Malle's predominantly sexist outlook. Towards the middle of *God's Country* Malle and his crew interview a young woman named Jean from Glencoe county. With cameras rolling Malle invites Jean to discuss her sex life, her status as a single woman, and what it is like to live in a conservative small town. At first Jean is pleased that a foreigner, a French filmmaker, is interested in her previously marginalised social experience. The opportunity to speak to camera is a chance for her to offer her

10 Todd Gitlin is here referring predominantly to episode six from the *L'Inde fantôme* series of films. A viewing of the scenes in question confirms his original judgement. In the same episode Malle's handling of the Indian Jewish community is equally troubling. Regarding that group Malle noted: 'There is something a little degenerate here. Something unhealthy. In this country where all the races are mixed-up together the jealous preservation by this community of the purity of its blood leads straight to the grave'. One imagines Malle would have later regretted this kind of statement. Gitlin was wise to tax him on these issues in his 1974 review. Let us also now note here that *L'Inde fantôme* provoked deeply hostile views from the Indian government and the British Indian community who attacked the BBC for supporting the film. Such was the controversy that the BBC was briefly invited to leave India.

viewpoint, to explain her struggles in coping with the social prejudices of a small town. This sequence was a genuine opportunity for
the mature Malle to move away from the dominant treatment of
women displayed in his earlier work ... Regrettably, the sequence
concludes as follows. With a touch of flirtation, Malle asks Jean: 'Is
sex important to you?'. Jean replies: 'I guess – I don't know. I guess if
I want to sleep with that person I will, but there's more involved. [she
laughs with more than a little embarrassment] I can't even talk about
this. I guess it's important, isn't it to everyone? [she laughs again]'.
Malle's film does not include a reply to Jean's pertinent question. The
conversation is suddenly stopped. Malle asserts his complete editorial
control over his documentary footage and moves on to show life in the
town hospital. I think this sequence is exemplary for a number of
reasons. It demonstrates how documentary too can be guided by
similar gender dynamics to the male gaze that is so operative in
narrative film. Here, Malle wants to watch his subject talk about sex,
to show to his audience a woman in an intimate moment, perhaps
also to display his own sexual attraction to her. But, his editorial
control does not allow the conversation to develop beyond these
parameters. Hypocritically, Malle will not respond to Jean's legitimate
question. The director's determining male gaze frames the interview
to such an extent that when the subject of his gaze becomes active,
enquiring and cleverly observant, socially interactive, Malle terminates
the sequence. Or as Mulvey originally noted of narrative cinema: 'the
male protagonist [here Malle himself as the offscreen voice in his own
documentary] is free to command the stage, a stage of spatial illusion
in which he articulates the look and creates the action' (1975: 13). Of
course, one could equally argue that Malle was editing the scene so as
to conclude with a dramatic rhetorical question to his audience, a
question that he perhaps felt was so obvious that it needed no answer.
Nevertheless, by the precepts of *cinéma direct* documentary film-
making the question that Jean posed to Malle merited a response. In
this instance Malle's silence is indicative of an inability to portray
women on equal terms to men in his cinema.

The passage from *God's Country* is just one further indicative
glimpse of Malle's residual masculinist outlook, his resistance to
thinking afresh on the portrayal of gender in his later films. Whereas
Malle did develop new and evolving political agendas, his representation of women remained relatively traditional in tone throughout

the filmography. For example, some years after *God's Country*, Anna
Barton (Juliette Binoche) from *Damage* (1993) is in many ways a
typical *femme fatale* who would not look out of place in either *Ascenseur
pour l'échafaud* or *Les Amants*. Unlike the story of Malle's political
evolution which I take up in the next pages no such developments
seem to change Malle's dominant characterisation of women. This
aspect of his cinematic discourse is a relatively constant feature.

Feminist film scholars have in many ways overlooked the cinema
of Louis Malle. However, his work represents a rich visual arena for
future study in the light of this theoretical perspective. More work is
required here, not least in the complex theoretical ground of gender
and documentary film. Malle's portrayal of women in that field strikes
me as being especially important (to an extent, one almost expects an
element of sexism in narrative film, it is a normal albeit unacceptable
part of the fabric of mainstream liberal fiction). Future research on
Mallean documentary, applying feminist and indeed also post-
colonial theory to *L'Inde fantôme*, promises an intellectually stimu-
lating project that deserves more time and space than I am able to
devote in this introductory study.

Le Souffle au cœur: breaking away and learning to laugh

While there are marked continuities in Malle's portrayal of women
throughout his career, a more changeable relationship develops in
Malle's later cinema regarding the politics of active pessimism found
in the films from the 1950s. After May '68 Malle's first major motion
picture for four years was the controversial hit, *Le Souffle au cœur*
(1971). As we know, it contested one of society's darkest taboos –
incest – and in so doing placed Malle at the forefront of early 1970s
cinema as a confrontational director prepared to test international
censors to their limits (for a more detailed contextual discussion see
Chapter 1 of this book). Notwithstanding the central theme of the
film, the historical setting of *Le Souffle au cœur* – '1954' – also represented an opportunity for Malle to look back on the era in which the
first phase of his career had developed. The new film allowed Malle to
criticise his earlier politics of active pessimism in the light of his new
post-May '68 position.

Le Souffle au cœur offers a subtle but critical view of the 1950s and to an extent also the director's own past. Every major social institution – including of course 'the family' appears to be in a state of collapse. The vision Malle pursues in *Le Souffle au cœur* is of a world in revolt – most notably between the three sons, Laurent, Thomas, Marc and their parents. Post-May '68 Malle is in little doubt as to which side he prefers. Consistently, his narrative and camerawork evoke sympathy for the young and against the old. Thus, when discussing the politicians in Paris and the conduct of the Indochina war, one of the boys undermines his father's comments by reminding him that he had voted for the government in the first place! Later when asked what he thinks about politics, the teenager Thomas declares: 'La jeunesse mon oncle, elle s'en fout!' ('Uncle, the young ... they don't give a damn!'). Similar acts of youthful revolt are lovingly played out across the film. A sense of anarchy runs through the family house and this is continued in the church where the altarboys pass messages to each other so as to arrange illicit opportunities to smoke cigarettes. Such episodes are each displayed by Malle in support of the younger protagonists and against the conservatism of the dominant adult powers. In short, Malle's 1970s vision of the 1950s is very different from his substantial work from that period (*Ascenseur pour l'échafaud, Les Amants, Vie privée* or *Le Feu follet*). Whereas in the earlier films Malle's focus had been on a mondaine world of indifferent adults struggling with their complex but sophisticated lives, Malle's *Le Souffle au cœur* sides with the arguments and frustrations of their children. Instead of focusing on the icy, pessimistic world of the bourgeoisie, Malle presents an ironic, burlesque, rough-and-tumble picture of growing up in confrontation with that class. Indeed, the picture is so brilliantly executed that it is easy to forget that Malle had once been closer to the adult world of bourgeois self-contempt than to the side of the teenagers that he now glorified. In that sense, the 1971 film revises Malle's own experience of the earlier decade and his political, psychological, emotional and cultural pose at that time.

It is of great importance to Malle's escape from the 1950s that the genre used to launch the rewriting of the 1950s was light comedy. This choice represents a bold break from the active pessimism that dominated his earlier work (notwithstanding *Zazie dans le métro*). In *Le Souffle au cœur* Malle deploys a withering variety of black humour. Let us look at one detailed scene from the film to see how this strategy is so powerfully executed. Much of what we see in *Le Souffle au cœur* is not always as it first seems, and this trick of comic inversion plays a strong element in the following passage from the film.

At the beginning of the film Laurent and another boy are idly collecting for an army charity that supports the victims of the war in Indochina. However, it quickly becomes apparent that most of the citizens of Dijon do not care for the soldiers at the front. Furthermore, we quickly learn that the boys are also prepared to exploit their role as budding patriots. So, when they enter a record store to search for the new Charlie Parker album, they use their civic activities to conceal their shoplifting of a new record. With a brisk jazz soundtrack playing, viewers are shown Laurent moralising to the reluctant shop-owner who complains about the number of charities 'these days'. The schoolboy record-thief Laurent replies: 'Mais, monsieur, il s'agit de la France' ('But sir ... this concerns France'). This passage is acutely ironic in the light of the cinematic codes used by Malle in his own first films. The schoolboys' actions are almost the complete opposite of the patriotic pessimism shown by, say, the character of Tavernier from *Ascenseur pour l'échafaud*. By 1971, Malle was cheerfully saying goodbye to the idea of war as a rite of passage. Gone is the 'myth of the paratrooper' that was central to work like the aforementioned debut film and the later *Le Feu follet*.

Comparable comic inversions to the scene that I have just described colour much of the rest of the film. However, in one superficially trivial scene Malle offers viewers and critics alike a clue to the wider strategy that I think he develops across the picture. Here, Laurent has been diagnosed with his heart murmur and his brothers bring litera-ture to his bedside. One of them announces: 'Proust pour distraire, Tintin pour l'instruire' ('Proust to distract, Tintin to educate'). As well as the apposite popular cultural reference to the 1950s comic strip hero, I think one can argue that Malle's film works with a similar switch of cultural codes as presented in this joke. Comedy is used by Malle to pursue a serious message. It instructs viewers that the social conservatism of the 1950s is on the brink of collapse. In its place all we are left with is the anarchic, jazz-scored world of the younger generation in which a son's sexual initiation by his mother is some-thing to be laughed at. In comparing Malle to Bernardo Bertolucci, Claretta Micheletti Tonetti argues that the French director's use of comedy in *Le Souffle au cœur* served to undercut the danger associated with filming incest. She explains: 'Malle's protagonists act in a moment of drunken euphoria, which the director in subsequent scenes tones down with liberating laughter, as if the matter should be ascribed to adolescent (and middle-aged) rebellion and remembered by the characters in question as something close to a joke' (1995: 172). The analysis displayed is plausible. However, in the context of Malle's earlier work the use of comedy in that film *was* a revolutionary gesture. The sound of laughter that recurs throughout the picture represents a powerful break with the aesthetics of right-wing romantic despair popularised by Malle in the 1950s and early 1960s. The comic lightness of touch displayed in *Le Souffle au cœur* marks the distance that Malle had travelled by the beginning of the 1970s. As if to confirm this rupture, film critics associated with extreme-right-wing politics who have praised *Le Feu follet* were disappointed in equal measure when it came to *Le Souffle au cœur* – a film that is for them only: 'pourtant fort médiocre' ('All the same, really mediocre') (de Comès and Marmin 1985: 72).

Conclusion

Malle never overtly rejected his past in his later films, for instance, the published script to *Le Souffle au cœur* is dedicated to Roger Nimier (Malle 1971: 5). Neither did he renounce the spirit of the decade in which he had launched his career. Similarly, as I have pointed out, the not so latent sexism of his handling of 1950s stars was never exchanged for a rhetorically more sophisticated approach as the years moved on or when he worked in the United States. However, I do think that Malle sought to move away dramatically from his earlier pessimistic sensibility and right-wing social contacts through the comedic tone that frames the impressive *Le Souffle au cœur*.

Nevertheless, continuities remain that suggest that the spirit of the 1950s was never entirely lost from view. Across his career Malle consistently opposed the bourgeois class from which he had emerged. Anti-bourgeois sentiment, or self-loathing, is recurrent throughout the oeuvre. Returning to the 1950s, let us recall, *Le Feu follet*. The power of this film today is surely found in its chilling depiction of loneliness and addiction in the modern city. It is an unremitting portrait of an outsider who is unwilling to conform to the capitalist–bourgeois society that was beginning to stabilise in early 1960s

France. Few directors have achieved a more challenging statement on the modern condition than Malle achieved here, irrespective of the political provenance of the film's literary source or its potential to be read as romantic treatise against decadence. Moreover, a similar outlook links films from *Le Voleur*, through *Le Souffle au cœur*, to *Pretty Baby* and some years later, *Milou en mai*. Malle's film-making of active pessimism and his later post-May '68 radical critique, are brought together by the withering eye he cast over the middle classes. This is a key element of unity that bridged the different stages of the director's political development, and an element that sits comfortably in both libertarian and fascist doctrine, blurring distinctions between traditional notions of left-wing and right-wing political traditions. With the passing of Malle, and Buñuel, it is also a current in French cinema that has become underrepresented, only perhaps being briefly recaptured in recent work like Céderic Kahn's *Ennui* (2000) or the Michel Houellebecq scripted, *Extension de la domaine de lutte* (1999).

And yet unravelling this part of Malle's cinema of ambiguity does not end here. Malle never utterly condemns the bourgeois world his camera seems so systematically attracted to. His cinematic imagination was composed of shades of grey, and the move towards the more radical agenda of *Le Souffle au cœur* only added to the shading. In that film the teenager, Laurent is asked by a young girlfriend: 'Cigare ou femmes?' ('Cigars or Women?'). He replies 'cigare' but then passionately embraces the woman who is next to him. Likewise, Malle positioned himself between fascination and disgust with the bourgeoisie, excitedly exploring and critically humiliating that class in equal measure.

Notwithstanding the thematic continuity of attacking the bourgeoisie, throughout *Le Souffle au cœur* Malle subtly implied that the 1950s had simply passed away into history and become the subject of his own black comedy. One might say that a bizarre historiographic game was at play. Malle's own cinematic career was in the process of rewriting its very origins. As we know Malle's fascination with his chosen medium's power to shape the historical record was far from over. In many ways it was just beginning. After *Le Souffle au cœur* his next fictional work, *Lacombe Lucien*, attacked the reassuring resistance mythologies of the occupation. It is to that film and the wider question of the role played by history in Malle's work that we will turn.

References

Beylie, Claude and Philippe d'Hugues (1999) *Les Oubliés du cinéma français* (Paris: Les Editions du Cerf).

Billard, Pierre (2003) *Louis Malle. Le Rebelle solitaire* (Paris: Plon).

Blondin, Antoine (1962) *Un singe en hiver* (Paris: La Table Ronde).

Blondin, Antonie (1964) 'Nous sommes Alain', in Henri Chapier, *Louis Malle* (Paris: Seghers): 170–2.

Blondin, Antoine (1991) *Œuvres* (Paris: Robert Laffont).

Borde, Raymond (1958) 'Ascenseur pour l'échafaud', *Les Temps modernes* April/May: 1908–10.

Bothorel, Jean (1993) *Louise ou la vie de Louise de Vilmorin* (Paris: Grasset)

Céline, Louis Ferdinand (1991) *Lettres à la NRF 1931–1961*. Etablie et presenté par Pascal Fouché (Paris: Gallimard).

Chardonne, Jacques and Roger Nimer (1984) *Correspondance 1950–1962* ed. Marc Dambre (Paris: Gallimard).

Dambre, Marc (1989) *Roger Nimier. Hussard du demi-siècle* (Paris: Flammarion).

Daniel, Joseph (1972) *Guerre et cinéma. Grandes illusions et petits soldats. 1895–1971* (Paris: Cahiers de la Fondation Nationale des Sciences Politiques).

de Baecque, Antoine (1997) 'Gégauff, le premier des Paul', *Cahiers du cinéma: Numéro spécial Claude Chabrol*: 88–91.

de Comès, Philippe and Michel Marmin (1985) *Le Cinéma français 1960–1985* (Paris: Editions Atlas).

d'Hugues, Philippe (1995) 'Roger Nimier au temps du "caméra-stylo"', in Marc Dambre (ed.) *Roger Nimier: Quarante ans après 'Le Hussard Bleu'* (Paris: Bibliothèque nationale de France): 231–44.

Drieu la Rochelle, Pierre ([1932] 1964) *Le Feu follet* (Paris: Folio).

Frank, Bernard (1952), 'Grognards et Hussards', *Les Temps modernes* December: 1005–18.

Gitlin, Todd (1974) 'Phantom India', *Film Quarterly* 27.4: 57–60.

Henley, Jon (1999) 'Cousteau was anti-Semitic and a Liar, says Biographer', *Guardian* 18 June: 17.

Hewitt, Nicholas (1996) *Literature and the Right in Post-war France: The Story of the Hussards* (Oxford: Berg).

Jackson, Julian (2002) *France: The Dark Years* (Oxford: Oxford University Press).

Malle, Louis and Daniel Boulanger with Jean-Claude Carviène (1967) 'Le Voleur'. English Translation of the script of the film; unpublished (British Film Institute Collections, London, England).

Malle, Louis (1971) *Le Souffle au coeur* (Paris: Gallimard).

Malle, Louis (1978) *Louis Malle par Louis Malle* (Paris: Editions de l'Athanor).

Malle, Louis and Marc Dambre (1989) 'Entretien exclusif avec Louis Malle', *Cahiers des Amis de Roger Nimier*, vol. 6: 5–17.

Malle, Louis and Philip French (1993) *Malle on Malle* (London: Faber & Faber).

Mulvey, Laura (1975) 'Visual Pleasure and Narrative Cinema', *Screen* 16.3: 6–18.

Nicholls, David (1996) 'Louis Malle's *Ascenseur pour l'échafaud* and the

Presence of the Colonial Wars in French Cinema', *French Cultural Studies* 7: 271–82.

Nimier, Roger (1950) *Le Hussard bleu* (Paris: Gallimard).

Prédal, René (1989) *Louis Malle* (Paris: Edilig).

Sellier, Geneviève and Ginette Vincendeau (1998) 'La Nouvelle Vague et le cinéma populaire: Brigitte Bardot dans *Vie privée* et *Le Mépris*', *Iris* 26: 115–29.

Sellier, Geneviève (2001) 'Gender, Modernism and Mass Culture in the New Wave', in Alex Hughes and James Williams (eds) *Gender and French Cinema* (Oxford: Berg), 125–37.

Tonetti, Claretta Micheletti (1995) *Bernardo Bertolucci* (New York: Twayne).

Vincendeau, Ginette (2000) *Stars and Stardom in French Cinema* (London: Continuum).

Violet, Bernard (1993) *Cousteau, Une biographie* (Paris: Fayard).

Weber, Eugen (1962) *Action Française: Royalism and Reaction in Twentieth Century France* (Stanford: University of Stanford Press).

4

Malle's histories

Lacombe Lucien has polarised critical opinion and sharply divided audiences in their views of Louis Malle. On the release of the film in 1974 critics on the left-wing of the political spectrum saw the work as a pernicious attack on the heritage of the resistance and the social struggle more generally. Malle's film had to be unmasked for what it was: a bourgeois manipulation of the historical record that normalised the banality of fascism and concealed the heroism and complexity of the class struggle (Foucault 1974; Daney 1974). However, for fellow director Joseph Losey, Malle's work was a masterpiece of the cinematic arts equal to Fellini's *8½*, John Huston's *Asphalt Jungle* and his own *Mr Klein* (see Caute 1994: 316).

In this chapter I do not want to be drawn further into the many controversial sub-debates that surround the political or artistic merits of *Lacombe Lucien*. Instead, I prefer to analyse how *Lacombe Lucien* works as a film, to discuss its core rhetorical devices and what they mean today. Here important comparisons will also be made with the equivalently ambiguous rhetorical strategies deployed by Malle in *Pretty Baby*. That film is important because it throws a powerful sidelight on the nature of Malle's better-known picture.

By way of an extended conclusion to this chapter my attention will turn to Malle's second American film, *Atlantic City USA*. Rather than marking a sharp break with Malle's preoccupation with history in work like *Lacombe Lucien* or *Pretty Baby*, it is a film that subtly re-enforces Malle's status as a memorial activist. It confirms and expands on his deserved reputation as a film-maker who repeatedly engaged with the meaning of the past.

'I can't bring myself to loathe you completely': the strategy of ambiguity in *Lacombe Lucien*

In the first instance, it is important to recall key details of the relatively straightforward plot of *Lacombe Lucien*. Lucien (Pierre Blaise) is an unpredictable, apolitical, violent and abusive youth. He is an arrogant and insecure teenager whom Malle shows lending his muscle to a band of small-town fascists in the final sultry days before the liberation. As Malle's film develops he shows us Lucien denouncing members of the resistance and tormenting a Jewish family that is hiding from the regime. Soon, Lucien is obsessed with the Jewish woman, France (Aurore Clément). His relationship with France is first pursued with naive charm. However, as France resists Lucien's advances he employs violence to dominate her. Thus, Malle's film is an intimate portrait of a single, provincial collaborator. Ultimately, in the final sequences of the work, Malle's camera follows Lucien, France and her elderly grandmother to the countryside where they wait for the conclusion of the war. The trio live happily together in a strange rustic playground that resembles a cross between a nostalgic eden and a science fiction utopia. Finally, with the sun shining brilliantly across Lucien's face, Malle informs his audience through a subtitle that Lucien was tried and executed by the resistance in the post-war purge.

Malle uses the opening scenes from *Lacombe Lucien* to introduce important and dominant aesthetic patterns that shape the rest of this work. As the film begins, Malle displays a text of white lettering on a black screen. The text reads: 'Juin 1944, dans une petite préfecture du sud-ouest de la France'.[1] Seconds later, the screen fades to a Catholic nursing ward, it is complete with two sisters clothed in white and grey wimples and walls elaborately decorated with crucifixes and other religious icons. Subsequently, Malle turns his camera to a boy who is cleaning the floor between the beds, the patients and their elderly visitors. The viewer's attention is next drawn back to a second figure that is positioned in the foreground of the shot. Here is another very similar adolescent who we see is busily engaged in his chores. He empties bedpans and mops the dull-coloured floor. To the far left of the screen, above one of the beds, Malle reveals a photograph of a military figure. Almost casually, Malle also shows the cleaner dusting

1 'June 1944, in a small *Préfecture* in south-western France.'

another photograph of the same face that is prominently placed on a small bedside cupboard. The portrait is a famous propaganda shot of Marshal Philippe Pétain, the head of the Vichy regime, the First World War hero, the Victor of Verdun. Malle allows his audience to notice that a rosary is casually draped around the frame of the picture.

Approximately two minutes into *Lacombe Lucien*, one of the nuns glances at her watch. She reaches up towards a prominently positioned radio that shares a shelf with a statue of the Virgin Mary. A voice from the radio declares that we are to hear a speech from Philippe Henriot,[2] entitled 'La revanche de l'histoire'('The revenge of history'). The sisters listen attentively as the programme begins but Malle's field of vision returns to the second cleaning boy. He has been distracted from his chores, seemingly not by Henriot's radio broadcast, but by a pretty yellow songbird that is perched on a branch outside the window. The adolescent takes aim with his sling shot. The bird is shot down. It falls to the ground, dead. In the background all the time the audience can still hear the voice of Henriot, who is now explaining that the resistance movement's propaganda is an insult to common sense. The camera lingers on the face of the adolescent assassin. He is a happy-go-lucky fellow, with wavy hair and a cheeky smile. Apparently oblivious to the radio broadcast, he turns away from the window and begins to mop the floor. Malle's camera records his movements from above and behind. Simultaneously, on the sound track we hear strains of a jazz tune. The overall effect is to establish sympathy with the young worker. The overhead camera angle and the combination of sunlight and the youthful movement of the mopping briefly implies an upbeat, cheerful and carefree tone. The sense of freedom that Malle now evokes contrasts with the conservatism of the hospital ward, the picture of Pétain and the monotonous droning of the lecture on the radio. Almost before we have time to map together these different images Malle takes his audience outside the building. We are swiftly transported into the countryside. The sun is still shining and one sees the cleaner-boy cycling through an idyllic rural landscape. He is free-wheeling down a beautiful hillside road. The jazz music that was hinted at seconds earlier is now far more prominent and it continues to play throughout this sequence without

2 Philippe Henriot, Vichy Minister of Propaganda, assassinated by the resistance in late 1944.

any further interruption. The Django Reinhardt and Stéphane Grappelli, 'Hot Club de France', music sounds wonderfully vibrant. A set of new white title lettering is placed against the shape of the cycling figure. This is 'Lacombe Lucien'. It is a 'Film de Louis Malle', with a 'Scénario de Louis Malle et Patrick Modiano'.

In the introduction to Malle's masterpiece several critical elements are displayed. Let us look at the first aspects of Malle's construction of his anti-hero in greater detail. In just three minutes of screen time Malle establishes a series of visual references that make Lucien exceptionally difficult for the viewer to place, to judge or to understand. At first Lucien potentially attracts audience sympathy. He is portrayed as a modest youth, working hard in unpleasant circumstances. It is almost by accident that he is drawn to our attention, after all he is the second young male figure that Malle shows his audience. Generally speaking, in these opening shots of Lacombe Lucien he is clearly presented as being far more attractive than the conservative institution in which he works. Moreover, Malle also implies that he is out of sympathy with his times, ignoring Henriot's broadcast that the sisters so attentively listen to. So, at first glance, Lucien looks very much like a victim of the Vichy regime, trapped in the hospital ward, where he is forced to dust the Catholic and Pétainist icons and to pour away the urine-filled bedpans that await his collection. However, Malle very quickly presents another far less attractive side to the teenager. It is for this reason that Lucien's bizarre attack on the songbird is important. Lucien's motiveless killing of an innocent bird disturbs our potential identification with him. However, almost as soon as it is presented, this negative depiction is suddenly withdrawn. Any sense of distaste towards Lucien evoked by the shooting of the bird is destabilised by the implicitly positive images of his rhythmic mopping of the floor and the first sounds of jazz music.

The first highly controlled pattern of representation that Malle imposes on Lucien becomes the central trope through which he is portrayed throughout the work. Malle resolves none of the contradictions through which he engulfed Lucien in the introductory sequence. Let us now discuss some further examples of the strategy to show its recurrence and deep resonance in the work. Indeed, it is by repetition of the initial framing motif that a dense pattern of ambiguity is created around the character of Lucien.

One of the most visually powerful scenes from Lacombe Lucien, I think, is when Malle shows Lucien's first morning in the employ of the pro-Nazi police. Here, one of the collaborationist policemen presents Lucien with a pistol and they engage in target practice. Lucien and his new colleague shoot their pistols at a poster of Pétain. Ironically, under the Marshal's wizened face the text of the poster reads: 'Etes-vous plus Français que lui?' ('Are you more French than him?'). The visual contradictions that are repeatedly associated with Lucien throughout the film are brilliantly displayed in this highly symbolic scene. On the one hand, Malle elicits audience sympathy through the powerful male bonding that is taking place between Lucien and his new mentor. Conversely, Malle has already let viewers know that Lucien's turn to collaborationism has resulted in the torture and death of a resistance fighter. Here, Malle makes us wonder which Lucien we should identify with: the former or the latter? Should audiences be repulsed by the malicious but bungling enemy of the resistance? Or, conversely, should they sympathise with the energetic young crack shot who is undergoing a classic cinematic rite of passage? The fact that Lucien fires his revolver at an image of leadership, conservatism and paternalism, Pétain, simply adds to the moral and political confusion that is rigorously constructed by Malle and his team. Visually and literally speaking, Malle films a symbolic act of resistance, but one that is nevertheless conducted by two characters employed in the service of the Nazi occupiers.

The point Malle is making in these scenes and many others is that one cannot bring fair judgement to bear on Lucien. Malle constructs Lucien as the embodiment of ambiguity and thereby as a site of prolonged visual fascination. The rhetorical structure of Malle's film does not allow plausible moral judgement of the character to be made. Instead, Malle constructs *Lacombe Lucien* around the repetition of contradictory presentations of its lead protagonist, and these are so densely woven that any balanced judgement is inherently problematic and unsustainable in the light of the permanently oscillating content of the film. Overtly signalling the underlying strategy again, several scenes later, the father of France, Monsieur Horn comments to Lucien: 'C'est curieux, je n'arrive pas à vous détester tout à fait' (Malle and Modiano 1974: 104).[3] Here, Malle places his vision of Lucien in the softly spoken words of Horn. Furthermore, due to the meticulous

3 'It's strange, somehow I can't bring myself to loathe you completely.'

consistency of Malle's characterisation of Lucien the statement *is* the only plausible one that can be made on the young collaborator. Malle does not let audiences completely hate Lucien. Just as importantly, he will not allow them to love him either. This, I think, is the central point of Malle's first film devoted to the period of the occupation. Following a line of argument appositely adopted by Richard Golsan, one can persuasively conclude that Malle frames *Lacombe Lucien* around a constant repetition of contradictions around how we are to read Lucien's behaviour (2000: 67–8; see also Higgins 1992: 204). As the British playwright Alan Bennett reminds us, such a consistent denial of moral judgement in characterisation and narrative is a rarity in cinema history. Bennett underlines Malle's achievement with the words: 'To have quite unobtrusively resisted the tug of conventional tale-telling and the lure of resolution seemed to me honest in a way few films even attempt' (2002: 16).

In fact, Malle hinted at the strategy I am discussing in the introduction to a collection of edited press reviews devoted to *Lacombe Lucien*. He offered the following explanation of his film:

> Il me semble qu'une des qualités du film est d'oublier les schémas et de présenter des personnages qui, par suite de situations elles-mêmes fort ambiguës, se voient amenés à exposer des contradictoires qui les font osciller sans cesse. C'est cette opacité même des personnages qui à permis tant d'interprétations contradictoires au nom de théories préconçues. (Malle cited in Raskin 1986: 3–4)[4]

As Malle admitted here, the core strategy of *Lacombe Lucien* is to prohibit the viewer from resolving the contradictions of the central protagonist. Any firm resolutions on Lucien are permanently deferred by the quality of his portrayal in the film. Malle and the brilliant performance from Pierre Blaise leave Lucien a polysemic figure. Provocatively, the strategy adopted in this work also chimes with one of Malle's more general, visceral comments on the nature of cinema per se: 'The spectator, alone in the world is a voyeur. He looks at the images, he adds his own fantasy, his mood of the moment, and makes

4 'It seems to me that one of the qualities of the film is its ability to forget schematic perspectives and to present the characters, who through the course of situations that are themselves highly ambiguous, are being exposed to contradictions that constantly oscillate. It is this very opacity of the characters that allows all sorts of contradictory interpretations to be placed on them, developed in the name of preconceived theoretical positions.'

them his own,' (BFI/Malle 1996). Through the strategy of ambiguity Malle forces us to make of Lucien what we can, to resolve his ambiguity by imposing our own fantasies.

Understandably, and correctly, much of the critical attention devoted to *Lacombe Lucien* has focused on its anti-hero. However, an equally ambiguous treatment of French history is also at play. Malle's more general strategy on the representation of history is visible and already at work in the opening sequences of the film that have been described above. This passage from the film is illustrative of the meticulous handling of the occupation period that runs throughout *Lacombe Lucien*. Following the initial indication of time and place, Malle shows his audience an immediately provocative artefact from the period: the photograph of Pétain, wrapped in rosary beads on the bedside table. In this single (about one second of film time) image Malle hints at the troubling link between the Catholic Church and the authoritarian Vichy regime. Through setting and detailed prop selection, Malle almost subliminally makes his opening statement on the history of the 1940s. The photograph of Pétain is in fact just the first of numerous other pointed background references in the film that represent the Nazi occupation. In *Lacombe Lucien* Malle works almost constantly to establish a disturbing series of snapshots of images of life under the Vichy regime. For example, among the many unexpected images of the period Malle shows in the film there are: a black French colonial helping the collaborators; Lucien's neighbour's brutal intimidations of his mother with gifts of toy coffins; and similarly, the disturbingly authentic anti-Semitic rhetoric that is placed in the mouth of Lucien's boss, the police chief. Malle introduces each of these nuanced details almost *en passant* during the course of his film. However, when taken cumulatively, they combine to disturb any safe or stable interpretation of the period. On the one hand, some of the details Malle included achieve calculated political insights, such as the highlighting of the complicity of the Church in the opening scene. Other examples work to generate an overall effect: the shock of the old. However, in this rich cloth of realist detail Malle rejects a single political thesis that might unify the meaning of his historical drama. Instead, a more fragmented puzzle is constructed by the director. In the course of his film Malle creates a new type of historical interpretation different from any of the more formal Pétainist, Gaullist, socialist or Communist accounts of the occupation that worked with more standardised, partisan stereotypes. The impact of the web of visually reconstructed historical details is to create a fictional film replete with subtle and implicit comments on the 1940s that confound audience expectations. Malle's representation of history is a profoundly revisionist ploy. The film is genuinely revisionist because Malle's mesh of contradictory references to the Vichy regime cast doubt on any of the more stable, ideologically consistent accounts of the period.

The very fabric of Malle's film disrupts any fixed interpretation of Lucien or the meaning of the historical backdrop in which his story is played out. The former aspect is yet another example of the strategy of ambiguity that frames much of the film. The 'revenge of history', to borrow the warning words from Henriot's radio speech that opened the film, that Malle wrought in *Lacombe Lucien* will therefore last for as long as viewers wish to puzzle over the moral status of the title character or to locate a political coherence in a historical backdrop that denies any simplistic interpretation. Thus, *Lacombe Lucien* also stands as a metaphor for Malle's own challenging and complex wider oeuvre that likewise consistently resists straightforward classifications. Lucien personifies Malle's repeatedly ambivalent positions, his contradictory relationship with the New Wave, his ambivalent intersection with the 'Hussards' novelists or his attraction to pessimism.

Having discussed the central filmic strategies at play in *Lacombe Lucien*, it is legitimate to ask what meaning can one ascribe to their use? Arguably, in the light of my reading of the politics of *Le Souffle au cœur*, Malle's strategy of ambiguity in the 1970s was open and libertarian in its motivation. His rhetorical stance implies a powerful and disturbing humanitarian gesture towards fascism that wishes to show that this movement was not exclusively composed of evil and insane monsters but included far more normal, ordinary individuals as well: men and women who were as politically unclassifiable as the likes of one peasant boy, Lucien. In short, Malle's position in *Lacombe Lucien* is most radical, stating: beware, under the correct conditions, anyone, but anyone, can become a fascist. This is a frightening but historically plausible position on the development of fascism in Europe. Drawing on the work of Kriss Ravetto (2001), it is also possible to see Malle's blurring of moral categories in the figure of Lucien as a means of undermining simplistic bourgeois notions of good and evil. Ravetto argues that this was the discourse at play in the comparable films of the 1970s by directors like Pier Paolo Pasolini (*Salò*) and Liliana Cavani (*The Night Porter*):

> the hyperbolic images of *Salò* – sadistic bourgeois fathers and aging femmes fatales made to look like drag queens – *The Night Porter* – repressed homosexual ballet dancers and former Nazis with monocles and SS uniforms hidden away in their closets ... cripple attempts to reemploy representations, monuments, and historical emblems in order to make a new subjectivity. Instead they compel the images of *einen Mann* (one man) and *richtigen Mann* (right man), as well as what Saul Friedländer calls 'Everyman' ... to appear ridiculous. As a result, they disavow collective subjectivities that rise out of the ashes of the traditional subjective communities predicated on moral values and national heroes, since these communities reinstigate xenophobic passions – that is hierarchies, segregations, racism and the erosion of singularities. (2001: 231–2)

Malle's strategy of visual ambiguity in *Lacombe Lucien* corresponds closely to the model Ravetto discerns in the films of Pasolini and Cavani. Malle's film's regime of ambiguity certainly denies all political certainties and frustrates their potential replication. Lucien's oscillations between heroism and villainy break down the veracity of either of these conservative categories. In this context, Malle's work is especially impressive for its subtlety. Unlike either Pasolini or Cavani's films, Malle achieves a comparable project without excessive screen violence or brutality. While some critics of Malle might see this aspect of his work as a weakness, as a residual bourgeois reliance on modesty, it is equally a unique signature that marks him apart from the Italian directors.

Nevertheless, the structure of ambiguity one finds in *Lacombe Lucien* comes at a high price. To measure fully the cost of Mallean ambiguity it is instructive to turn briefly to Malle's third period film from the 1970s, *Pretty Baby* (1978). *Pretty Baby* shares a similar sense of ever-shifting viewpoints as that found in the more successful *Lacombe Lucien*. In this, his first American film, Malle presents his viewers with a perplexing set of discourses regarding child prostitution–sexuality. On the one hand, Malle consistently implies that Violet's (Brooke Shields) life as a prostitute in turn-of-the-century New Orleans is a painful and disturbing experience. For example, in probably the most powerful scene from the film, when Violet's virginity is auctioned to the highest bidder in the brothel, Malle's cinematography strongly suggests that we are witnessing a brutal bourgeois hypocrisy. Here, the Mallean cinematic eye shows his audience the rich, well-dressed town-fathers of New Orleans salaciously looking at the victimised child. As Malle's camera slowly moves from male face to male face an implicit condemnation is offered. There is a genuine sense of indignation here. Conversely, in a typically ambiguous flourish, Malle does not pursue the above approach with any consistency. Instead, Malle establishes a counter-discourse that is quickly juxtaposed with the former perspective. Now, Malle implies that in Violet and Bellocq's 'marriage' a kind of brief moment of libertarian happiness is achieved. This tone is especially dominant in an important sequence towards the end of the film. Bellocq and Violet have been married and together with their friends from the brothel they drive to the banks of the Mississippi to celebrate. The sun shines, a jazz tune is played over the sequence, and Malle suggests that a kind of idyllic interlude is at hand. Furthermore, to underline the mellow mood Malle injects a passage of humour to the scene. A boat full of workmen sails past Bellocq and the prostitutes on the riverbank, and suddenly the men from the boat swim across the river to meet them. The group is shown to be laughing together and one of the workers exclaims to Bellocq: 'You are the luckiest guy in the world'.

The oscillating perspectives that I describe in *Pretty Baby* are highly reminiscent of the approach identified in *Lacombe Lucien*. Indeed, in balancing off 'bourgeois hypocrisy' with the utopian Bellocq–Violet relationship (albeit at times nuanced and moderated), Malle was offering a most dangerous and provocative discourse to the wider cinema-going public. Notwithstanding nuance or other visual caveats that are introduced, scenes like those on the riverbank tend to glorify a criminally abusive relationship. Here, Malle's constant desire to avoid conventional moral judgement ran the risk of lapsing into a different kind of unforgivable judgement by default. This tendency, the ambiguity, the balancing of judgements, is surely misplaced in the light of the genuine experience of the victims of abuse, an experience that is never fully explained by Malle's excessively neutral and repetitive photography of Violet's bittersweet eyes. Nor for that matter is it addressed in his retrospective justifications of this film. Commenting at the time of the film's British release Malle explained: 'I've been accused of exploiting her, but that's not true.' 'She used me.' (cited in *Now* magazine 1979: 118). This is one Mallean inversion that stretches credibility to breaking-point.[5]

What are the lessons of *Pretty Baby* for our understanding of *Lacombe Lucien*? Importantly, the former film shows the social and political dangers that are at play in the Mallean strategy of ambiguity. The introduction of a discourse of ambiguity in the context of fascism and collaboration is no less perplexing than its use regarding childhood sexuality. Just as in *Pretty Baby* there is an implicit reluctance to think about the victims of abuse, so here there is, generally speaking, a piecemeal denial of the victims of fascism. While of course under the ambiguous discursive style there is a condemnation of Lucien's activities in Malle's work, there remain those other scenes in which his life is partially glamourised. Marie Chaix's reaction to one such scene of this type, captures the problem. She asserted: 'Quand *Lacombe Lucien* mâchonne un brin d'herbe dans une douce clairière, l'œil glissant sur le beau corps de la 'petite juive' ... j'ai envie de vomir' (Chaix cited in Friedländer 1982: 131).[6] In presenting the innocent, ordinary side to fascism, or the charming side of paedophilia, Malle inevitably mitigates the suffering of the victims of these phenomena. Therefore, what Malle's films leave the audience with are questions of redemption. Who are we to redeem? Lucien? Bellocq? Or, ultimately, also Malle for constructing these ambivalent fictional characters in the first place? No number of viewings of either of the Malle films will bring an answer to these questions, they are just too ambiguous, so the point really is that viewers are invited by the strategy to make their own judgements.

Finally, there is a further caveat regarding the rhetoric of ambiguity found in *Lacombe Lucien* and *Pretty Baby*. Paradoxically, while the strategy implies that a viewer has free rein over how to interpret the balance of content in the films there is also a more

5　This is not the only sexist and dated remark Malle made at the time of *Pretty Baby*. Malle's otherwise very informative interview with *Literature/Film Quarterly* (1979) contains especially honest and uncomfortable comments on E. J. Bellocq's photography and Lewis Carroll's relationship with children (93-4). Readers are invited to read the original source and make of it what they will. Of course, like the filming of *Lacombe Lucien* Malle's statements on *Pretty Baby* were often calculatingly ambiguous and thus do not easily permit critical condemnation.

6　'When *Lacombe Lucien* chews on a blade of grass in a soft forest glade, his eye slipping on to the pretty body of the little Jewish girl ... I want to vomit.'

hegemonic side to the rhetorical stance. The impact of Malle's technique of implicitly saying everything (condemning and forgiving; presenting two mutually exclusive political theses simultaneously in one film) is a position of great power and authority. It is a hegemonic ploy because through its usage Malle controls the complete visual/ rhetorical content that is offered in his films. In that sense Malle only invites viewers to make up their own minds on the basis of the illusion that he has presented all the options, which inevitably he has not. This tension is unavoidable and inherent in the discourse Malle enjoyed using by the mid-1970s. Malle probably appreciated the intractable dilemma of his own rhetorical position, just as one senses that he identified with the predicaments of his all his major protagonists from Tavernier in *Ascenseur pour l'échafaud* to Uncle Vanya in *Vanya on 42nd Street*.

Spiralling ambiguity: *Lacombe Lucien* and the *mode rétro*

The aesthetic patterns we have discussed in *Lacombe Lucien* fall squarely into the wider *mode rétro* fashion in literature, art and cinema that developed in western Europe at around the end of the 1960s. This term refers to those many west European films that challenged previously conventional ways of depicting the Third Reich and the Second World War (see Friedländer 1982). Everything about the subject matter and plot of *Lacombe Lucien* confirms the piece as a central *mode rétro* film. In this work Malle codifies fascism through the fashionable 1970s themes of sexual violence and fantasy. Specifically, the trope of a fascist–Jewish sexual relationship, playing with political and sexual power games, also looks typical of that era's wider cinematic handling of similar material. In making *Lacombe Lucien* Malle was partially tapping into the new international trend for all things related to sex, fascism, Nazism and the 1930s. Or, as Susan Sontag memorably explained at the time: 'Now there is a master scenario open to everyone. The colour is black, the material is leather, the seduction is beauty, the justification is honesty, the aim is ecstasy, the fantasy is death' ([1974] 1996: 105).[7]

7 Even Malle's soundman, Jean-Claude Laureux, was not immune to the wider mood. His directorial contribution in this period was *Les Bijoux de famille* (1975). Although an 'erotic' film, later released on video in Britain under the title *French*

As my brief summary suggests, films like *The Night Porter* (Cavani 1974) or *The Damned* (Visconti 1968) were replete with visual and political ambiguities. However, perhaps the most hidden and fascinating paradox of the cultural movement, and Malle's contribution to it, is more subtle. *Lacombe Lucien* and the *mode rétro* offered a new discourse on fascism, collaboration and the 1930s. However, at the same time, deeper cultural paradigms were also being restaged. As I will now explain one cannot simply argue that the new mood for filming fascism in the 1970s style was utterly original. In fact, a blurring of innovation and tradition is at play. Certainly, in the case of *Lacombe Lucien* longstanding and influential antecedents are evoked.

As Roderick Kedward notes, Malle had been close to cultural contexts in which collaboration had already been widely treated long before 1974 (Kedward 2000: 234). For example, the anti-resistance novels of Malle's friend Roger Nimier frequently looked at the politics of the 1940s with a sarcastic, violent and wry tone. Figures such as Sanders from his *Hussard bleu* offer early sketches of ambiguous collaborators who unlike Lucien reinvented themselves as war heroes. A further key intertextual precedent is the Jean-Louis Curtis' novel, *Les Forêts de la nuit* (1948). As Kedward explains: 'set in a small town in the south-west of France, [it] features the drift into collaboration by the sexy young Philippe Arréguy, and his seduction of the refined and resistance-minded daughter of the nobility, Hélène ... Philippe must have been at least an unconscious model for Lucien' (2000: 234).

Other important portrayals of collaborationism from the French literary canon similarly paved the way for Malle's later film. Distinctive forerunners to the film are to be found in Jean Genet's *Journal d'un voleur* (1947) and *Pompes Funèbres* (1953). In particular the latter book offers a dazzling portrayal of homoeroticism and collaborationism among German and French youth at the time of the

---

Blue, Vichy still hovers in the background. A poster of Pétain apparently looks down on the more central sexual gymnastics on display. I have not had the opportunity to watch Laureux's work. The descriptive details I owe to a brief review from *Positif*, no. 169 (1975): 65 and *Video Business* 5.10 (May 1985): 38. Coincidentally, the film was produced by Vincent Malle with Films Français de Court Métrage. To date, research does not suggest that Louis Malle was involved in his colleague's controversial debut. Vincent Malle also produced the better-known spectacular, *La Grande Bouffe*, Robert Bresson's *Lancelot du lac*, as well as several of his brother's films.

liberation. There is also a relatively famous short story by Jean Cau that was published in Sartre's review, *Les Temps modernes* (1952). Entitled 'La Vie d'un SS Français' it was in fact, according to Edmund White, a free adaptation on the life of one of Genet's lovers, "Java"' (White 1994: 358). Quoting Java, White underlines the fact that he never regretted his service in the SS. Java stating in the 1980s: 'I am only sorry we lost' (cited in White: 359). In the light of the above intertextual reference points, one is not surprised to discover that Malle had initially thought of involving Genet in the writing of the *Lacombe Lucien* script (see Billard 2003: 337–8).

Apart from literary intertexts that anticipated Malle's film, the cinema also foreshadowed the breaking of taboos surrounding the portrayal of collaboration. As Henry Rousso and Jean-Pierre Jeancolas have uncovered, a previous picture from the early 1960s had already presented a similar narrative to *Lacombe Lucien*. The film in question was Kerchbron's *Vacances en enfer* (1961) and rather like Malle's later work it too focused on the misadventures of a young collaborator on the run (Rousso 1990: 264; Jeancolas 1979: 213). Less directly related to *Lacombe Lucien*, other works from the late 1950s and 1960s also anticipated the spirit of the film from the early 1970s. As I explained in the previous chapter, there is a haunting presence of right-wing anti-heroes in New Wave cinema and Fourth Republic film more generally. Typical examples are to be found in Claude Chabrol and Paul Gégauff's *Les Cousins*, as well as in Jean-Luc Godard's, *A Bout de souffle* and *Le Petit soldat*. Malle's own portrayals of Tavernier and Alain in *Ascenseur pour l'échafaud* and *Le Feu follet* are not such distant relations from the later Lucien. These films and their male anti-heroes, arguably, also contributed to the construction of a socio-cultural framework out of which *Lacombe Lucien* would later emerge. Moreover, Malle (1989: 157), Pierre Billard (2003) and Maud Cognacq (2002) relate *Lacombe Lucien* directly to the war of decolonisation in Algeria. They see prototypes for Lucien in the young officers forced to fight in North Africa. Similarly, Malle had also spoken of a desire to work on the subject of police gangs operating in contemporary Mexico City which influenced his thinking on the film (Malle and French 1993: 90–1). In fact, Malle was sometimes keen to list almost every reactionary group from the post-war period as having been part of his vision for Lucien: 'I became more and more intrigued by these insignificant, banal fascists ... My project had its roots in the wars successively, in Algeria, Latin America, and Vietnam' (Malle 1989: 157). Elsewhere Malle has also suggested that his film was loosely inspired by his own terrible childhood experiences of the Second World War (Malle and French 1993: 98). However, as we know, he did not offer a directly autobiographical representation of that period until some fifteen years later in *Au revoir les enfants*.

One must also recall a more direct influence on *Lacombe Lucien*, the NEF- produced film by Robert Bresson, *Un condamné à mort s'est échappé* (1956). After *Le Monde du Silence*, Malle had briefly worked as an assistant director to Bresson on this film and it is here that one finds the most graphic antecedent to *Lacombe Lucien*. During a question and answer session on a visit to the National Film Theatre, London, Malle explained that Robert Bresson had telephoned him after watching *Lacombe Lucien* (1974). The fellow director wanted to know if Malle's 'Lucien' was indeed the same character that had appeared in his own film, the figure of 'Jost'. In *Un condamné* he is a young deserter from the German army who is thrown into the same prison cell as the lead protagonist, the resistance fighter, Fontaine. Suddenly, Fontaine's detailed plans for escape are placed in jeopardy. In Bresson's film we gradually see that this schoolboy collaborator will assist in the resistance fighter's flight from prison. Visually speaking, 'Jost' looks very much like 'Lucien' and they are of about the same age and stature. Both boys are also shown to have drifted towards Nazism. Speaking on this coincidence in London, Malle accepted that his memory of 'Jost' must have subconsciously influenced his casting of Pierre Blaise in his film. The Bresson scholar Keith Reader explains: 'Fontaine's doubts about Jost's reliability – concretized by his turning up in the cell wearing a mixture of French and German uniforms – certainly suggests a possible resemblance between the two characters that goes beyond the merely physiognomic' (Reader 2000: 47). The diametrically opposite behaviour of Bresson's 'Jost' and Malle's 'Lucien' confirm Reader's suspicion regarding the similarity between the protagonists. In Bresson's film the haphazard apolitical former collaborator is redeemed by his assistance in the resistance escape plan. Here, Jost loses his initial political ambiguity and very clearly chooses sides. In counterpoint, in a famous scene from *Lacombe Lucien*, Lucien is presented with a similar opportunity to redeem himself, to become a 'résistant', and to escape his tragic fate. As one would expect on the basis of Malle's strategy of ambiguity

Lucien flatly rejects the 'Jost option' of unambiguous redemption. Far more wilful and complex than Jost, Lucien is shown by Malle to be simply irritated by the resistance fighter and his mistaken use of the 'tu' form of address in their conversation. Instead of redeeming himself, Lucien silences the man by placing a sticking plaster over his mouth and the Mallean strategy of ambiguity is allowed to continue. Thus, Malle's scene inverts the Bresson intertext and the inversion suggests that a deeply symbiotic relationship is at play between the two films. Provocatively, one might ask if Malle was suffering from what Harold Bloom has called the 'anxiety of influence'? Malle was a great admirer of Bresson, and the scene implies that he was simultaneously paying homage to a father figure while attempting to break free from his influence. In the light of this evidence the originality of *Lacombe Lucien* is further nuanced.

Two more contemporary reference points from the 1970s must also be highlighted: the films of Bernardo Bertolucci and the fiction of Malle's script-writer, Patrick Modiano. It seems to me that *Lacombe Lucien* owes a special debt of thanks to the cinema of Bernardo Bertolucci, in particular *The Spider's Strategem* (1970) and *The Conformist* (1970). Both works strongly foreshadow the key feature of Malle's film and remind us that his work was not simply emerging out of a uniquely French cultural context. Four years before *Lacombe Lucien*, in *The Spider's Strategem*, Bertolucci problematised standard political–historical (socialist, liberal or conservative) interpretations of the 1930s and 1940s. In so doing Bertolucci presented an utterly ambiguous character: an Italian resistance hero who paradoxically had also been a traitor to the cause. Furthermore, later in the same year, Bertolucci's *The Conformist* provides a second key intertextual reference point to Malle's film. Starring Jean-Louis Trintignant, it is one of the first films to focus entirely on a figure with quasi-fascist political affiliations. Like Malle, Bertolucci made audiences watch the often violent and repugnant behaviour of a confused young fascist for the length of an entire feature film.

The immediate forerunners to *Lacombe Lucien* provided by Bertolucci in 1970 are important because they established a contemporary cultural space to which Malle would also contribute. In this respect Malle and other French film critics have been wrong to overlook the influence of the Italian director in favour of the role played by the documentary *Le Chagrin et la pitié* (directed by Marcel

Ophuls in 1972 and distributed by Malle's NEF group). Of course, that documentary on the Nazi occupation of Clermont Ferrand is also an important work in preparing the way for Lucien's arrival on the screen. However, it can only be a matter of French cultural jingoism to ignore the comparable influence of Bertolucci. For what it is worth, critical discussions of Bertolucci's cinema tend equally to repress the figure of Malle (see Tonetti 1995). I suppose this mimetic negation is to be expected with each director and their critical supporters denying the other the critical space that they merit.

The script-writer, Patrick Modiano, is the final key protagonist in the conception of *Lacombe Lucien*. Like Bertolucci his contribution to the development of Malle's film is critical for several reasons. First, it is evident that *Lacombe Lucien* transposes significant elements of the novelist's contemporary fiction to the screen. In particular, the band of collaborators that Lucien joins are comparable figures to the burlesque characters that populate Modiano's early fiction (see for example, Modiano, 1968; 1972). Similarly, there is something equally Modianoesque about two characters from *Lacombe Lucien*: M. Horn and his daughter, France. The fact that these hidden Jews have links to the local French Nazi police echoes passages from the disturbing world of Modiano's writing in which national, political and religious and cultural identities are terribly blurred. Thus, collaboration with Malle offered Modiano an opportunity to show off his already contro-versial literary vision to a wider audience.

Once more in the study of Mallean film, a paradoxical picture emerges. Certainly, films like *Lacombe Lucien* and much of the rest of the *mode rétro*, marked a sea change in the public representation of Vichy, Nazism and the 1930s to 1940s. However, *Lacombe Lucien* evidently also emerged out of several, deeper literary and filmic reference points that pre-dated the 1970s. *Lacombe Lucien* did not appear from a cultural vacuum. Instead, a cultural tradition, running from Nimier to Genet, and onto Malle and Modiano, via Italy and the work of Bertolucci, found a greater space within the cultural main-stream than ever before. In *Lacombe Lucien* Malle brought a previously relatively marginal set of cultural and political discourses together in a new synthesis that found access to a wider public than had previously been possible.

Reviewing the cultural context also helps identify more clearly what was original about Malle's Lucien. First and foremost there is the 'pure' Frenchness of the character, his rural roots, and all the local colour that is offered in the film. That is very distinct from, say, Bertolucci's *The Conformist*, a film that is broadly set in Rome and only partially in Paris. Generally speaking, the setting used in *Lacombe Lucien* stands out from all of the cultural antecedents I have discussed. Susan Sontag's *mode rétro* 1970s master narrative of black leather and sado-masochism is essentially an urban kind of kitsch. Malle did not indulge in that aspect of the scenario and *Lacombe Lucien* gains in originality for that. Similarly, while films like Bertolucci's *The Spider's Strategem* anticipate Mallean rhetorical postures, Malle's film remains distinctive. In particular, Malle's broadly realist presentation of an ambiguous teenager is some distance from the more overtly playful *nouveau roman* narrative adopted by Bertolucci. In *The Spider's Strategem*, the ambiguity of history is presented through an elaborate non-linear narrative structure of flashbacks and flashforwards. Malle's work achieves a similar visual frisson but predominantly via the rhetorical presentation of the character of Lucien. Malle's strategy is in some ways a stronger cinematic approach because it wears its colours more lightly and so is less likely to be subject to cultural fashion effects. Likewise, Malle's creation of an absolutely ambiguous anti-hero moves his work closer to Modiano's oeuvre and slightly away from the world of Roger Nimier's earlier fiction. This is the last ambiguity that I want to conclude with regard to *Lacombe Lucien*. Just as with *Le Souffle au cœur*, *Lacombe Lucien* represents as much a break with the Hussard tradition as it does a silent debt of thanks.

New Mallean history: *Atlantic City USA*

After *Lacombe Lucien* and *Pretty Baby* the past continues to feature in Malle's work even when it is least expected. Despite the fact that *Atlantic City USA* is set in the present (the early 1980s) it underlines how Malle was a director who was utterly at home questioning the legacies of history. This film is especially important because it highlights a movement in Malle's work away from the direct historical reconstructions found in *Lacombe Lucien* and *Pretty Baby* towards a more overtly psychologically informed questioning.

Atlantic City USA is a crime story involving a drugs theft and the mob's attempt to recover its illicit property. The film is set in 1979 and on the surface at least there is little to do with history in the material. This is only part of the story. Ghosts from the city's past are repeatedly evoked by Malle in a film that becomes a delicate study of nostalgia. The character of the ageing gangster Lou (Burt Lancaster) personifies the theme. His conversations with the young hippie-thief, Dave (Robert Joy), and lady friend, Sally (Susan Sarandon) are filled with a love of the past. For example, he muses on the 'good old days' of the 1930s and 1940s when the city was booming and its criminal underworld had its own code of ethics and role to play in the casinos. Talking to his young companion David, Lou recalls: 'It's all shit now. Now it's all so God-damn legal ... It used to be beautiful, the Atlantic Ocean was something then. You should have seen it then. You should have seen the Ocean in those days'. These phrases capture the tone of bitter-sweet nostalgia that recurs throughout *Atlantic City USA*.

Critics publishing in *Cahiers du cinéma* did not see much depth to Malle's new North American work. Rather dogmatically it seemed to them that the *rétro* director of *Lacombe Lucien* fame was up to his old bourgeois tricks again. Sarcastically summing up in a short review that was part of 'Notes sur d'autres films', one reads: 'Une photo dans le style Hamilton accentue le côté rétro et sucreries d'*Atlantic City*. Cela se regarde avec la même nonchalance qu'on feuillette un magazine de tourisme dans un drugstore' (Lardeau 1980: 53).[8] However, a fresh viewing of *Atlantic City USA* suggests that Malle's film has far greater depth than the 'glossy magazine' *rétro mode* perceived by the *Cahiers du cinéma* critic. Malle is not simply offering a conservative take on nostalgia. In point of fact, there is something far more complex at stake in this work. Importantly, as the film develops it quickly becomes apparent that Lou's nostalgia for 'old time' Atlantic City life conceals a far darker presence of the past in the film. Much of the narrative tension of *Atlantic City USA* hinges on Lou's psychological relationship with a repressed episode from his history. Gradually, as the plot develops, we learn that Lou is haunted by the fact that in his youth he failed to rescue one of his friends during a shoot-out and that as a consequence of his (in)actions a tragic

8 'Notes on Other Films'; 'Photography in the Hamilton style accentuates the sugary *rétro* side to *Atlantic City*. It looks at itself with the same nonchalance of flipping through a tourist guide in a drugstore.' It is remarkable to note that as late as the 1980s the *Cahiers* critics indirectly still describe Malle's privileged childhood through the use of the adjective 'sugary'.

death occurred. Malle portrays Lou as being haunted by his failure to assume the role of a hero. His gangster clothes and muscular tough guy postures belie a deep sense of personal failure. Malle's film is therefore essentially about Lou's attempts to rewrite his tragic origins. The work is therefore not an exercise in the superficial *rétro* key. Instead, *Atlantic City USA* is a meticulous and thoughtful study of its central protagonist's psychological obsession with history. Thus, in the concluding scenes of Malle's work audiences witness Lou gradually reconstructing the dynamics of his earlier tragedy. For example, when his lover (Susan Sarandon) is threatened by a hood wielding a gun, Lou intervenes and in shooting down the aggressor he revises his moment of historical shame. A small personal victory seems to have been wrought. For the almost constantly pessimistic Malle this is perhaps the best one can expect from life, an opportunity for a second chance.

Atlantic City USA stands out then from the earlier 'history' films from the 1970s. To an extent the ambivalence and ambiguity of the earlier work is now replaced by the more familiar meta-narrative of trauma, repression and re-enactment that anticipates themes raised more explicitly in *Au revoir les enfants*. When compared to *Lacombe Lucien* or *Pretty Baby* Malle's engagement with history here has moved to the ethically and politically more reassuring ground of psychoanalysis. The core of Lou's story and Louis Malle's film is the working through of a repressed trauma. Nonetheless, shadows of the earlier ambivalent discourse found in *Lacombe Lucien* linger on in the characterisation of Lou. For example, while Malle implies that Lou's second chance to act, to shoot the mobster dead, releases him from his shame it is equally evident that Lou's act of psycho-historical reconstruction is still tied to the past. Malle shows us that Lou feels that he is now a real hero, but his redemption is utterly entwined with his original sin. If *Lucien* were the personification of good and evil in the body of one country boy from the south-west of France, then here Malle celebrates and pities Lou's murderous intervention in equal measure.

Notwithstanding the retention of these ambiguities, *Atlantic City USA* reverses the underlying narrative conceits employed to frame *Lacombe Lucien* and *Pretty Baby*. In those films Malle dramatised two troubled childhoods, exploring the dynamics of the traumatic experiences of a young peasant and a 12-year-old girl. Malle's treatment of Lou is a simple inversion of this perspective. In *Atlantic City USA* he enters the world of the adult and takes up the question of the legacy of a traumatic history. Here we are not concerned with the facts of Lou's original youthful indiscretion but rather its longer-term psychological implications. For the scholar of Mallean film this change in direction is an important and original shift of gear. It means that *Atlantic City USA* is a film that more closely anticipates later work of a similar key, films like *Damage* (1992), than it replicates the angle adopted in the four previous films from the 1970s.

The handling of the psychological legacies of history in *Atlantic City USA* anticipates many of the discussions of Mallean cinema that are thrown into greater relief in the light of *Au revoir les enfants* (1987), Malle's later account of his own traumatic history from the Nazi occupation of France. That film and the wider subject of trauma in Mallean cinema will be dealt with in detail in the next chapter. For now, it is sufficient to underline the fact that Malle did not abandon his thematic interest in history after the completion of *Pretty Baby*. If anything *Atlantic City USA* provided a different but equally rich canvas through which to explore the relationship between history, character and psychology.

Conclusion: the film-maker as a memorial activist

The political historian and barrister Serge Klarsfeld uses the term 'militants de mémoire' (memorial activists) to describe those groups in contemporary France who actively campaign for recognition of historical wrongs conducted by the French state under Vichy and in subsequent conflicts (Klarsfeld and Bochurberg 1997: 9). Used with a different emphasis, the same expression encapsulates the spirit of Malle's engagements with history as displayed in *Lacombe Lucien*, *Atlantic City USA* and elsewhere. Malle made films that he knew would disturb audience assumptions about history, the most notable example being *Lacombe Lucien*. He also produced work that reflected on the more complex problems of historical change, the personal experience of psychological trauma. These films show the hallmarks of a director whose passion was to investigate and to explore; to offer ideas and questions; to provoke thought. The epithet 'memorial activist' is also appropriate to Malle for a further reason. Not only did his films aim to overturn conventional ways of interpreting episodes from history but they also represented the past through innovative cinematic forms. Films like *Atlantic City USA* stand out as examples of how cinema can bring a new purchase to the genre of history by exploring the psychological meaning of the past without redress to the sumptuous but hollow reconstruction work of a period drama. It is a mark of Malle's ingenuity that films like those we have been discussing conform exactly to Robert Rosenstone's definition of postmodern historical cinema (reflexitivity; contradiction; open-endedness; multiplicity of viewpoints) (1995: 206–7) without betraying the dominant aesthetic modes I discussed in Chapter 2 of this book.

Lest we should be in any doubt about Malle's versatile fascination with the historical, let us briefly consider the final scene from *My Dinner with André* (1981). The film is a bravura of experimental filmmaking. It is also a thoughtful philosophical exercise and satirical commentary on the banality of intellectual pomposity (see King 1997: 111–24). However, Malle's film, and Shawn and Gregory's original stageplay, conclude on a moment of great poignancy. The less practical but clearly wealthier protagonist, André, pays for the sumptuous dinner and this means that Wally can now afford a cab journey home to his partner Debby. Strangely elated after so much intellectual activity in one evening Wally stares out from the window of his cab. As the grim city lights flash by we hear his thoughts:

> I rode home through the city streets. There wasn't a street – there wasn't a building that wasn't connected to some memory in my mind. There, I was buying a suit with my father. There I was having an ice cream soda after school. When I finally came in, Debby was home from work, and I told her everything about my dinner with André. (Shawn and Gregory 1981: 45)

In this final, quietly emotional scene Malle resolutely asserts a powerful defence of the importance of the past. In sharp contrast to the figure of Lou in *Atlantic City USA*, Wally finds great solace in the streets he knows, the experiences he remembers. In the light of Malle's earlier engagements with historical material that I have been discussing I think that this scene is a beautiful touch. In it I like to think that Malle is suggesting that despite the troubling qualities of his earlier 'history films' the past is still not necessarily a place to be afraid of. After the controversies of his work on collaborationism, his uneasy treatment of paedophilia, Malle offered glimpses of the therapeutic power of recollection. For once in Mallean cinema here is a past that heals. The passage does not paper over the edginess of the previous films. In its distinctive difference of emphasis it throws them into greater relief.

Notwithstanding my enjoyment of the last moments of *My Dinner with André* a final issue must now be discussed. In this chapter I have implicitly argued that while *Lacombe Lucien* generated controversy its content is perhaps easier to come to terms with today than the discourse on children, prostitution and sexuality Malle offered in *Pretty Baby*. That film and some of the comments that Malle bandied at the time of its release are at the very least dated and at worse an elaborate apology for male fascination with younger teenagers. Until now this part of Malle's career has been glossed over. The popular critical literature on Malle does not discuss this matter in any detail (Malle and French 1993; Billard 2003). Furthermore, few film critics or theorists ever discuss any of Malle's work from America, let alone the troubling history of *Pretty Baby*. Occasional references are made to Susan Sarandon's participation in the film, but no one recalls the historically more significant 'Brooke Shield's phenomenon', the mass-media frenzy that surrounded the sexualised 'girl-star' in the late 1970s and early 1980s, the *Vogue* covers, the Calvin Klein advertisements or other perplexing controversies. One major reason for this lack of critical uptake is that *Pretty Baby* is certainly a difficult film for mainstream audiences to come to terms with. By Malle's standards it was also a relatively weak work. Moreover, since the late 1980s, Malle's popular reputation has become so closely related to *Au revoir les enfants* that it seems almost incongruous to debate *Pretty Baby* at all. It is in this way that one of Malle's most troubling works has been lost.

So, there is an important consistency across Mallean cinema. The filmography has a strange propensity to rewrite its own meaning. First, the right-wing politics of the 1950s are reinvented through the comic retrospective, *Le Souffle au cœur*. Subsequently, the implicit dangers of 1970s libertarianism are likewise skirted around. Just a handful of informed feminist scholars have started to pick over the handling of women in the oeuvre. Subsequently there is the case of the forgetting of *Pretty Baby* that I have outlined above. In that way Malle's filmography displays a recurrent but unnerving talent for reinvention and self-repression, with film after film neutralising the provocations of its predecessor. That is a further feature of this director's legacy. Mallean film almost constantly sweeps aside its last contribution in favour of creating a new controversy in which the earlier material is repressed. It is in the next and final chapter of this study that I analyse the wider question of repression in Mallean film. Much of his work displays a repressive tendency and this is an issue that is best understood in the light of *Au revoir les enfants*.

References

Anon. (1979) 'Pretty Baby', *Now Magazine* 14 Sept.: 116, 118.

Bennett, Alan (2002) 'Seeing Stars', *London Review of Books* 24.1 3 January: 12–15.

Billard, Pierre (2003) *Louis Malle. Le Rebelle solitaire* (Paris: Plon).

Cau, Jean (1952) 'La Vie d'un Français SS', *Les Temps modernes*: 2032–43.

Caute, David (1994) *Joseph Losey: A Revenge on Life* (London: Faber & Faber).

Cognacq, Maud (2001) '*Lacombe Lucien* et Louis Malle: portrait d'un film au regard de l'histoire' MA dissertation; supervised by Olivier Dumoulin, Lettres et Sciences Humaines, University of Rouen.

Curtis, Jean-Louis (1947) *Les Forêts de la nuit* (Paris: Julliard).

Daney, Serge (1974) 'Devenir Fasciste', *Libération* 7 Feburary: 1.

Foucault, Michel (1974) 'Anti-Retro', *Cahiers du cinéma* 251/252 (July/August): 5–15.

Friedländer, Saul (1982) *Reflets sur le Nazisme* (Paris: Seuil).

Genet, Jean (1953) *Œuvres Complètes* (Paris: Gallimard).

Golsan, Richard J. (2000) *Vichy's Afterlife: History and Counterhistory in Postwar France* (Lincoln, NE: University of Nebraska Press).

Higgins, Lynn (1992) 'If Looks Could Kill: Louis Malle's Portraits of Collaboration' in Richard Golsan (ed.) *Fascism, Aesthetics and Culture* (London: UPNE): 198–211.

Jeancolas, Jean-Pierre (1979) *Le Cinéma des français. La Ve République 1958–1978* (Paris: Stock).

Kedward, Roderick (2000) 'The Anti-Carnival of Collaboration. Louis Malle's *Lacombe Lucien* (1974)', in Susan Hayward and Ginette Vincendeau (eds), *French Film: Texts and Contexts* (London: Routledge): 227–39.

King, W. D. (1997) *Writing Wrongs: The Work of Wallace Shawn* (Philadelphia: Temple University Press).

Klarsfeld, Serge and Claude Bochurberg (1997) *Entretiens avec Serge Klarsfeld* (Paris: Stock).

Lardeau, Yann (1980) 'Notes sur d'autres films', *Cahiers du cinéma* 316 (October): 53.

Malle, Louis and Patrick Modiano (1974) *Lacombe Lucien* (Paris: Gallimard).

Malle, Louis (1974) *Audio Tape Interview from the National Film Theatre, London* (London: BFI).

Malle, Louis (1979) 'Creating a Reality that Does not Exist: An Interview with Louis Malle', *Literature/Film Quarterly* 7.2: 86–98.

Malle, Louis (1989) 'Afterword', in Louis Malle and Patrick Modiano, *Au revoir les enfants and Lacombe Lucien* (London: Faber & Faber).

Malle, Louis and Philip French (1993) *Malle on Malle* (London: Faber & Faber).

Malle, Louis and 'the BFI' (1996) *Louis Malle: A Celebration of his Life and Work: Commemorative Programme* (London: BFI Special Collections).

Modiano, Patrick (1968) *La Place de l'étoile* (Paris: Gallimard).

Modiano, Patrick (1972) *La Ronde de Nuit* (Paris: Gallimard).

Raskin, Richard (1986) *Lacombe Lucien* (London: BFI).

Ravetto, Kriss (2001) *The Unmaking of Fascist Aesthetics* (Minneapolis: University of Minnesota Press).

Reader, Keith (2000) *Robert Bresson* (Manchester: Manchester University Press).

Rosenstone, Robert (1995) *Visions of the Past* (Harvard: Harvard University Press).

Rousso, Henry (1990) *Le Syndrome de Vichy. De 1944 à nos jours* (Paris: Seuil).

Shawn, Wallace and André Gregory (1981) *My Dinner with André* (London: Methuen).

Sontag, Susan (1996) 'Fascinating Fascism' in *Under the Sign of Saturn* (London: Vintage).

Tonetti, Claretta Michelleti (1995) *Bernardo Bertolucci* (New York: Twayne).

White, Edmund (1994) *Genet* (London: Picador).

5

Primal scenes

This chapter focuses on *Au revoir les enfants* (1987). The film is especially critical to our knowledge of Malle's work because its content implies that one can reinterpret Malle's artistic output as a long struggle with the memory of his traumatic childhood experiences suffered under the Nazi occupation of France.

Psychoanalytic interpretation of *Au revoir les enfants* reveals many important insights, not least those suggested by Lynn Higgins in her discussions of Mallean cinema and the primal scene (1992: 198–211). However, I will also demonstrate that Malle is too complex to be explained by one theory or interpretation, however tempting its conclusions. Other forms of psychoanalytic reading, not so directly related to trauma or the idea of the primal scene, can be applied. Notably, Freud's notion of *Das Unheimliche* ('the uncanny') is an important intertextual reference point. Likewise, in the concluding pages of this chapter I return to a more politically informed consideration of *Au revoir les enfants*. Here, I will delineate the libertarian critique that Malle offered in this film. Arguably, it is one of Malle's strongest and most successful interventions.

Four decisive hours in a child's life

Before examining *Au revoir les enfants* in any depth it is helpful to present the historical–biographical context Malle reflected on when making his film. This is important because the work is the most overtly autobiographical of Malle's films. It is also unlikely that readers will be fully apprised of the precise details that form the backdrop to the later dramatic reconstruction.

For the 11-year-old Louis Malle, 15 January 1944 was probably going to be another mundane Saturday of classes in his still relatively new boarding school, the Petit Collège des Carmes. Located near to Fontainebleau, on the outskirts of Paris, the Petit Collège was a logical place to house a child in a time of war and political confusion. It was for precisely this purpose that Malle's parents had sent him to this rural outpost of Catholic education. However, by approximately 10 o'clock that January morning the relative tranquillity of the safe haven was shattered. Malle, his school, its pupils and masters, were suddenly catapulted into the violence and cruelty of the occupation and Nazi genocide. German forces, Gestapo officers and ordinary Wehrmacht soldiers, executed a raid in search of hidden Jewish children.

Briefed by an unknown informer, the soldiers targeted several specific classes, including Louis Malle's fifth-grade group. In the middle of a lesson, two Gestapo officers broke into the room and abruptly interrogated the group. The Germans called out the name of one pupil who they believed to be Jewish and to be hiding in the class under an assumed identity. The name that the German shouted out was 'Bonnet' and after calling it twice, Jean Bonnet (the alias used by a German Jewish boy, Hans-Helmut Michel) stood up and surrendered himself. According to Malle's later memory of the event Bonnet then tidied his books and made a tour of the classroom, passing among his colleagues, shaking their hands and saying 'Au revoir Malle ... Au revoir Boulanger' (Malle 1978: 14; Malle cited in Guérin 2000: 465–6). Three broadly comparable scenes to the one I am describing were played out in other classrooms of the school.

Within one hour of the start of the raid, the Nazis forcibly moved all the children attending the college outside their classroom into the yard. Terrified and cold, no doubt shivering and sweating from fear in the winter air, the pupils discovered that their head teacher, the priest, Père Jacques had been arrested. Next, a Gestapo officer treated the children to a humiliating lecture. Just a few months later this scene was recorded in a privately printed review devoted to the history of the college, *En famille ... quand même* (1944) (key extracts from which are reprinted in Braunschweig and Gidel 1989: 36–7; see also Carrouges 1988: 175–6). The officer began with a question to the children:

'Trois élèves juifs ont été arrêtés dans ce collège; y-a-t-il encore des Juifs parmi vous?'

Ce à quoi les élèves répondent ensemble: 'Non'.

Un élève, P. de la Guiche, réplique: 'On ne savait pas qu'ils étaient juifs.'

Ce qui a le don d'exaspérer le chef de la Gestapo, qui crie: 'Vous le saviez'.

'Ce sont nos camarades, comme les autres'. S'écrie un élève de seconde, Germain de Montauzan.

L'Allemand répond: 'Vous n'êtes pas camarades avec un nègre, vous n'êtes pas camarades avec un juif.'[1]

This vile rhetoric was soon exchanged for a more physical, ritualistic form of abuse. The historical documentation suggests that a soldier called out the surname of each pupil from the school. Without any explanation, on hearing their name the Nazis required each pupil to walk towards the wall of the chapel. We know from the same school yearbook that describes these events that the first name to be called out was Aussenard. Terrified at being moved apart from the group, Aussenard stood by the chapel wall fearing for his young life, visibly shaking as he awaited his fate. Slowly, the other boys rejoined him, one by one, as each responded to the German soldier's orders. Since the exercise was probably conducted in alphabetical order one can plausibly presume that 'Malle' must have been barked out roughly at the middle point of the register. While this brutal process followed its unremitting alphabetical logic the captured children, including Bonnet, were marched past their colleagues. Bonnet appeared bruised from a beating that he had already received at the hands of his captors. A few minutes later, the Nazis escorted Père Jacques from the institution. As he passed his former pupils he bravely said a good-bye. The group responded together with a similar greeting.

Perhaps angered by the children's courage and loyalty the Germans released a guard dog to run among the boys. In response they remained standing in silence next to the chapel wall. During the role call the

[1] 'Three Jewish pupils have been arrested in this college; are there any more Jews among you?' To which the pupils replied together: 'No'. One pupil, Pierre de la Guiche replied: 'we did not know that they were Jews.' A reply which seemed to exasperate the head of the Gestapo who cried out: 'You knew.' 'They were our friends, just like the others,' cried out a sixth former, Germain de Montauzan. The German replied: 'You are not friends with a negro, you are not friends with a Jew.'

Nazis divided the boys into separate subgroups of four. Presumably this was a standard Nazi strategy to maintain order and to assert complete symbolic domination over prisoners. The report in the school yearbook underlines a further act of heroism. One pupil, Pierre de Laguiche, kicked the dog. In retaliation the Gestapo officer hit de Laguiche four or five times in front of his young colleagues. The officer subsequently shouted out to the other pupils: 'Vous faites du mal à un pauvre animal ... c'est donc "l'élevage" que vous recevez dans ce collège' (cited in Braunschweig and Gidel 1989: 37).[2] The tension was broken a little. The boys had noticed the Nazi's misuse of the French language which was ironic in the light of his new-found interest in national educational standards. Nonetheless, the school was closed by later that day and Malle's attendance at it had been brutally suspended.

It remains in doubt as to precisely which Nazi officers were directly responsible for these actions. In one report of the raid, reference is made to an officer who is named as 'Turrel from Danzig' (*En famille, quand même*, [1944] cited in Braunschweig and Gidel 1989: 36). In contrast to this assessment other accounts of the episode have emphasised the role of the Gestapo agent for the Melun region, Sergeant Wilhelm Korf (Braunschweig and Gidel 1989: 115; Malle has also sometimes referred to a German called Kopf, with a 'p', in his accounts of the episode. See Malle cited in Guérin 2000: 466; likewise a Korf(f) is cited as the key figure in a third historical description of this episode found in Carrouges 1988: 175. Despite the linguistic slippages it is plausible to accept 'Korf'). Korf was tried before a French military tribunal in 1953 for a different but comparable attack on a Catholic institution. Despite being condemned to death Korf's sentence was commuted to imprisonment. However, as the post-war years unfurled, the authorities granted amnesties as former Nazi war criminals were reintegrated into new civilian lives. Korf was released from prison in 1960, the same year that the still relatively young Malle collaborated with Jean Paul Rappeneau and Volker Schlöndorff on a first colour feature, *Zazie dans le métro* (Braunschweig and Gidel 1989: 116).

2 'You are doing harm to a poor animal ... so that is the "breeding" that you receive in this school.' Note: here the German officer misuses the term 'élevage' which literally means rearing or breeding.

The bureaucratic ruthlessness of the persecutors of the Holocaust means that the records of their victims are meticulously documented. The three boys that the Nazis took from the school, Hans-Helmut Michel (alias Bonnet), Jacques Halpern and Maurice Schlosser were deported to Auschwitz. We also know that Hans-Helmut Michel was sent to the death camp in convoy number 67, leaving from the Paris holding-camp Drancy (Braunschweig and Gidel 1989: 3). Neither he, Halpern nor Schlosser survived. The Nazis eventually released a fourth boy who had also been taken in the same round-up. They had designated him as an Aryan and he was consequently returned to his family. Père Jacques, the resistance fighter, who had used his institution as a sanctuary for children fleeing anti-Semitic persecution, did not survive the war. The Nazis deported him to Mauthausen-Gusen concentration camp, in Austria, where his treatment resulted in his death. Each of these micro-historical decisions tellingly reveal the logic of genocidal racism.

During the occupation of France, Nazi and Vichy authorities deported eleven thousand children to their deaths (Klarsfeld and Bochurberg 1997: 230). Their suffering and that of approximately one and half million other Jewish children murdered in the course of the Holocaust was a long and protracted process. The story of the hidden children is one of sudden friendships, hopes raised and then instantly crushed. For Jewish children across Nazi-controlled new Europe there was first the pain of separation from their parents as they were desperately placed in hiding. Subsequently, there was the inevitable disorientation of flight and unpredictable clandestine existence. Eva Fogelman explains just one common experience: 'They witnessed naked men, women, and children – among them their own relatives – lined up and machine-gunned in town squares and in the outskirts of cities ... The imminence of their own deaths was pervasive' (1993: 293).

Au revoir les enfants: film and the representation of catastrophe

The final fifteen minutes of Malle's film dramatise many of the historical scenes I have just documented. *Au revoir les enfants* is in fact a work predominantly about school life under the Vichy regime. The picture is a touching but tragic portrayal of one class, Malle's own, and their experiences of the vagaries of wartime existence. Thus, Julien

Quentin (Malle's filmic alter ego) is sent back to the countryside school by his mother. Slowly, the new term brings new experiences and lessons. There are of course the banal classes in mathematics, literature and Greek. As Malle's plot develops we watch Quentin encounter a new boy in his class, Jean Bonnet (alias Jean Kippelstein, in historical reality Hans-Helmut Michel). The dynamics of this relationship shape the rest of the work. Gradually the two boys become friends: Julien, who is fascinated by Bonnet slowly learns that he is a hidden Jew. As the friendship grows Quentin loses his confused childhood prejudices towards the Jews. Subsequently, the relationship is abruptly halted by the Nazi raid. Malle's work concludes with the dramatic scene of Père Jean (based on the real-life Père Jacques) saying good bye to his pupils. Seconds later the adult Malle asserts via voiceover that he has never been able to forget this period of his life.

It is all too easy to understand *Au revoir les enfants* as Malle's attempt to reintegrate a childhood trauma into his adult life. History, autobiography and film-making come together in this work to form a site for a painful but curative 'working-through.' This perspective is the overwhelming implication of the final minutes of Malle's film. Here, in the voiceover from Malle, one dominant meaning of the film is asserted. Quietly, but firmly, Malle underlines his fidelity to the terrible episode from his youth. He explains: 'Bonnet, Négus et Dupré sont morts à Auschwitz, le Père Jean au camp de Mauthausen. Le collège a rouvert ses portes en octobre 1944. Plus de quarante ans ont passé, mais jusqu'à ma mort je me rappellerai chaque seconde de ce matin de janvier' (Malle 1987: 132–3).[3] Malle's incisive but simple words carry great authority as they recall the essential facts of this single episode from the Holocaust. In addition, they highlight Malle's own deep and complex loyalty to his formative childhood experience and then also project it forward to his own anticipated death. The voiceover functions as a reintegration of the historical trauma into the contemporary life of the director. By concluding *Au revoir les enfants* in this way Malle had found a new sense of moral purpose in his cinema. This statement is an original example of unambiguous

3 'Bonnet, Négus and Dupré died in Auschwitz, Father Jean in the camp at Mauthausen. The school reopened its doors in October 1944. Over forty years have passed, but I will remember every second of that January morning until the day I die.'

political and ethical duty towards a formative disaster. Certainly, in just a limited period of film time Malle's voiceover organises his work into a coherent and moving narrative on memory, loyalty and attempted closure.

Much of the content of *Au revoir les enfants* problematises the dignified but reassuring conclusion to the work. In particular, Malle's handling of the development of the key relationship between Julien Quentin and Jean Bonnet is replete with suggestive material. As Lynn Higgins has argued, through the exploration of Julien Quentin and Jean Bonnet's friendship Malle addressed a 'primal scene' from his youth. The key scene to which Higgins refers is at the heart of the tragedy: the Nazi raid on Quentin and Bonnet's class. Here, Malle portrays his schoolroom as a site of danger, betrayal and guilt. A Nazi officer, Müller, walks slowly between the wooden tables and demands whether there is a Jewish child in the classroom. The officer turns his back from the children for a moment, he dismissively plays with a war map that is on the wall, and in that split second, Malle shows Quentin glancing back at Bonnet. Out of fear, friendship or fascination, we watch the Mallean alter ego betray his new friend. So, in the blink of an eye, Quentin is presented as partially responsible for the arrest of Bonnet. Persuasively, Higgins explains: 'I submit that it is this moment of Julien's glance that constitutes the primal scene, or in Lifton's words, the "residual image – the pictorialization of [the individual's] central conflict in relationship to the disaster" that haunts the narrator in the final voiceover, presumably Malle himself' (Higgins 1992: 207).

Here, Higgins is arguing that Malle's wartime experience has come to haunt his later career as a film-maker and that in *Au revoir les enfants* he is finally publicly revisiting the founding episode. The interpretation that Higgins offers does not refer to the classic Freudian primal scene, in which the child observes his or her parents during sexual intercourse (see Freud's writing on *The Wolf-Man*). Instead, she reapplies the same term to identify the impact of a non-sexual, violent and traumatic episode from Malle's childhood. Or, as Emma Wilson has slightly more cautiously described the same scene: 'this moment, this involuntary glance is the film's *raison d'être*' (1999: 97).

Quentin's betrayal of Bonnet foregrounds the importance of guilt in Malle's work. This aspect is repeatedly hinted at throughout the film by Malle's recurrent use of similar scenes of guilty glances between the boys. The first appearance of the theme is offered when

Bonnet is introduced to his new class (Malle 1987: 21–3). As the teacher drones on about the qualities of Charles Péguy's poetry Malle briefly includes a shot of Quentin looking back across the room towards Bonnet. It is almost exactly the same image as the later primal scene to which Higgins refers. The links between this first and last encounter are further highlighted by Malle. In scene seven (the first look) a noise from outside the classroom disturbs the boys. A German soldier has arrived in the schoolyard and is talking to a monk. This shot prepares the way for the betrayal, violence and guilt that will follow. The fact that Malle repeats the exchanges of looks and glances between Quentin and Bonnet throughout the film adds to this implicit psychoanalytic subtext that is finally played out in the afore-mentioned primal scene of Bonnet's capture. The subtle redundancies in *Au revoir les enfants* work up to the final scene of denunciation. On the one hand, this repetition confirms Higgins' thesis. One would exactly expect to see a recurrence of versions of a traumatic or primal scene before its full execution. However, visually speaking, the repeti-tions of looks and glances between the boys also nuance the meaning of the primal scene. Inevitably, when it takes place, it is one further example of the common relationship that Quentin and Bonnet share. Repetition makes Quentin's last fatal glance almost an instinctive, accidental betrayal.

Since Malle informs us in the *Malle on Malle* interviews that he did not in fact give Bonnet away, the guilty looks in the film are not to be taken literally (Malle and French 1993: 179). Instead, they each reflect a more general shame on Malle's behalf. Or, as Higgins again underlines: 'The story is not a confession for a wrongdoing, rather it is invented to account for the guilt' (1992: 211). One might go on to say that the centrality of guilt in Malle's film adds a deeply critical quality to the work. It brings the question of how to respond to the meaning of the Holocaust directly into a retrospective filmic representation of the Holocaust. Malle conducts this exercise without trivialisation or glib reconciliation.

Nevertheless, as we should by now know, Malle rarely provides work that falls neatly into unambiguous, analytical categories. One must underline the fact that *Au revoir les enfants* contains another, supplementary scene of looking and denunciation that is as sugges-tive as the passage we have been discussing. In the later scene from the film, Malle reverses the roles earlier ascribed in the 'primal scene in the classroom'. Thus, in the middle of the Nazi raid, Malle shows Julien Quentin in the school hospital ward trying to save one of the other hidden boys. A German soldier arrives in the ward and at first thinks that Quentin is another clandestine Jew. Subsequently, Malle shows the German soldier force Julien Quentin to lower his shorts to establish whether he is circumcised. Seconds later, the nun, who stands by watching this symbolically sexual attack on Quentin, nods towards one of the other boys who is hiding in a nearby bed. The soldier captures the boy and leaves. One of the resistance priests arrives in the ward and subsequently Quentin looks at the nun with complete contempt. He cries out: 'C'est elle', she replies: 'Foutez le camp!'(– 'It was her'; – 'Go to hell!') (Malle 1987: 127).

In these dramatic passages from the film, Malle inverts the dynamics of the earlier scene from the classroom. Now, Quentin is presented as the subject of the German soldier's visual interrogation. Here, Quentin endures his humiliation without giving away the boy who is hiding in the ward. Finally, as the German soldier exits, Malle allows Quentin to adopt the gaze of a resistance fighter: casting his eye on the nun and accusing her of betrayal. What I think Malle is doing in this part of the film is producing a troubling postscript to the earlier classroom episode. In short, he is deliberately problematising the former classroom scene's status as the 'primal scene', the defining episode through which to interpret his work. In his decision to invert that earlier scene Malle is suggesting that the experience of the Nazi raid meant that one did not have time 'to be guilty', or 'to be innocent', to behave well or badly, to think, or to feel anything other than fear. Chaotic events simply took place and a child could show great cowardice and courage within a matter of seconds of each other. Experiencing such adult brutality meant that for bystanders and victims all psychological and moral positions were thrown into turmoil. In episodes like those that concluded *Au revoir les enfants* betrayal and heroism went hand in hand. In these moments of history anything could happen and that was what was so terrifying for a child who was used to a more ordered world. A similar discourse to Malle's work frames much of Roman Polanski's more recent treatment of the Holocaust, *The Pianist* (2002). As a perceptive critic has noted of that film, Polanski's greatest achievement is found in his depiction of the entirely arbitrary nature of life and death during the Nazi genocide (Frappat 2002: 76–7). Malle's earlier dramatic reconstruction of the two scenes from the round-up precisely anticipates Polanski's later more extensive representation.

One could also argue that the hospital ward sequence that I am raising for attention here represents *the key* Mallean primal scene. The scene includes several elements that do seem critical to Malle's work and that are absent from the classroom sequence. Here, Malle includes the implicit questioning of his own identity; in turn, this is related to the question of circumcision and genital–religious–racial identity. Furthermore, the figure of the nun is cast as a female voyeur witnessing Malle's own humiliation. Speculatively, Malle's prolonged interest in childhood sexuality could be interpreted as a slow processing of this type of terrible encounter, a desire to return to this scene, to repeat it. Similarly, his tendency towards misogyny is also anticipated, but not justified, in the role played by the woman in this episode, with Malle transferring his own guilt to her. Perhaps too Malle's deeper guilt does not revolve around the question of the act of scopic betrayal but rather the guilt that he was not identified as a Jew, and hence not taken in Bonnet's place? This would in turn be closer to the guilt of a survivor rather than of a voyeur turned collaborator. At the very least, the hospital scene includes the key figures of a terrifying family unit: soldier/resistant as authoritarian father, nun as punishing mother, and Quentin/Malle as child. However, an alternative reading of this passage, more in line with Higgins' original thesis, is equally plausible. One can interpret the second hospital ward scene as a rapid re-enactment of the original classroom episode, with the guilty Quentin now unburdening his earlier shame onto the nun.

Familiarity with Malle's wider work provides further insights on his decision to film the same style of scene twice over in *Au revoir les enfants*. In this context, the presentation of Quentin as first guilty in the classroom and subsequently heroic in the hospital ward looks like that favourite Mallean strategy of ambiguity so consistently applied in *Lacombe Lucien*. The strategy pays off whenever it is used because it quickly creates ambiguity and poetic richness. Importantly, it allowed Malle to say the same thing in different ways and with different variations of political, social or moral emphasis. The technique brings depth and sophistication, while astutely avoiding precise repetition. The strategy also cleverly protects Mallean film from simplistic critical analysis.

It is now productive to move away from the idea of the primal scene in Malle's film to an equally intriguing line of psychoanalytic enquiry. The fact that two relatively similar scenes are filmed closely together by Malle raises the wider question of duplication and doubling in Malle's cinema. These ideas are the subject of Freud's work on the *Unheimlich* – 'the uncanny' – (1919). Certainly, 'the double' or *Doppelgänger* forms a powerful thread in Mallean cinema and also seems to underpin the repetitions I have been discussing in the context of *Au revoir les enfants*. Throughout Mallean film twins implicitly form single or complementary social outlooks: Wally and André from *My Dinner with André*, as well as earlier the two Marias from *Viva Maria*. *Lacombe Lucien* offers a comparable but different variation. Here the idea of the 'double' is captured in a single protagonist with Lucien embodying two different value systems: good and evil. The apogee of Malle's filming of the double is *William Wilson*, the adaptation of Edgar Alan Poe's *Doppelgänger* short story. Wilson is the literal 'uncanny double' of folklore and horror fiction. In the light of this feature of Mallean cinema one could run an argument that suggests that Quentin and Bonnet from *Au revoir les enfants* are a further pairing in the series.

What does the visual and narrative propensity to use the figure of the double in Mallean film mean? Potentially, it is the presence of 'the double' in Malle that is the defining projection of an inner psychological melodrama. Here, Freud's original hypothesis on the double in his work on 'the uncanny' supports the hypothesis. For Freud the phenomena of the uncanny is explained as follows: 'this uncanny is in reality nothing new or alien, but something which is familiar and old established in the mind and which has become alienated from it only through the process of repression ... the uncanny as something which ought to have remained hidden but has come to light.' ([1919] 1985: 361–2) So, this would mean Malle's doubles, his repetitions, twins and split-personality anti-heroes, are manifestations of a struggle to repress or to accommodate a childhood trauma. Each of the second figures representing a shadowy projection of a memory that will not quite go away.

Alternatively, as Nicholas Royle suggests, when working with a reading of Jacques Derrida's interpretation of the uncanny, there is something about the creative process which is always intrinsically about a question of doubling (2003: 198). Royle asserts that in the act of writing there is always a duplication – the written 'I' in the text, and the writer sitting at his or her table. I do not think it is a disservice to Royle's thesis to see an equivalent process at work with a literary film-maker like Malle. With Malle, there is always the 'I' of the director, behind the camera or at the editing suite, and more often than not there is also the 'I' of the character in the autobiographical films, in this case Julien Quentin. Indeed, Malle is so often doubly present in his work: as director and projected central protagonist. Among the many *Doppelgängers* to choose from there are Malle and Alain Leroy/ Maurice Ronet (*Le Feu follet*); Malle and Georges Randal/Jean-Paul Belmondo (*Le Voleur*); Malle and Laurent/Benoît Ferreux (*Le Souffle au cœur*); and finally, to repeat, Malle and Julien Quentin/Gaspard Manesse (*Au revoir les enfants*).

Malle's repeated emphasis on Julien Quentin's scopic power, his fascination with, and objectification of, Bonnet, of course quickly raises a further key question. Astutely, Lynn Higgins asks whether Malle's obsession with watching and looking, the strong element of voyeurism in *Au revoir les enfants*, indirectly comments on Malle's adult career as a director. Higgins states: 'The figure of the fatal glance ensnares the profession of filmmaking as well, here the traumatic memory, "pictorialized" as a guilty glance, offers an insight into Malle's vocation as a filmmaker. Is the making of fictional images symptomatic of a repressed trauma that gets repeated and transformed as it inevitably returns?' (1992: 210). The implication of Malle's film, his recurrent emphasis on identity and looking, strongly implies that this is precisely the case. Moreover, the fact that much of Malle's oeuvre displays a similar fascination with the power of the look/camera, adds supporting evidence in favour of Higgins' conten-tion. In fact, if one reviews Malle's films then anticipations of 'the look' later deployed more fully in *Au revoir les enfants* are everywhere. Malle's brief and repeated portrayals of a child witnessing a disturbing act look like a signature motif in many of his films. One might begin a survey with *Ascenseur pour l'échafaud*, where a little girl approaches the building in which the murderer is trapped in the lift. Likewise, Malle shows youngsters playing outside Alain's asylum in *Le Feu follet*. What do they accidentally witness as they look into the garden of the private clinic? There are many other comparable cases. However, the sharpest anticipation of the theme of the look offered in Mallean cinema is found in *Black Moon*. Its opening sequence offers a series of 'scenes of witness' where Lily sees the mayhem and murder produced by the fantasy sex-war that haunts Malle's dream-film. In short, voyeurism and the objectifying power of the look, are emphasised throughout Malle's work, from *Ascenseur* to *Damage*.

Freud's work on the uncanny, to which I have already referred, also offers an alternative interpretation of the recurrent 'looks' in *Au revoir les enfants*. Here, Freud's discussion of 'the evil eye' (*der Böser Blick*) is relevant. He recalls that in folkloric superstition there are many examples of understanding looking as a way of bringing harm, giving the evil eye. This issue is clearly relevant to understanding Malle's filming of Quentin's visual interrogations of Bonnet. Freud explained the evil-eye phenomenon as follows: 'Whoever possesses something that is at once valuable and fragile is afraid of the other person's envy he would have felt in their place. A feeling like this is betrayed by a look even though it is not put into words' ([1919] 1985: 362). The analysis works well with *Au revoir les enfants*. Malle is potentially implying that Quentin's glances at Bonnet are a form of the evil-eye relationship. From this perspective they would represent the disturbing fact that Quentin knew that in Hitler's Europe, and Pétain and Laval's France, he held a terrible advantage over the Jew Bonnet. It is because Quentin cannot cope with the guilt that this power brings that he recurrently casts his glances at Bonnet. Thus, it is Quentin's fear of being envied that is relieved through the act of visual aggression. So, Bonnet is now placed not only at the mercy of his racial–political enemies (the Nazis/French fascists) but also in the hands/eyes of his shamed Gentile schoolfriend. And, if one agrees with the above interpretation, then one inevitably also senses that Malle's film completely understood the terrible psychological implications of living in Nazi Europe. This is an insight that goes well beyond the parameters of Malle's own retrospective assertion of his memory and guilt offered at the conclusion of *Au revoir les enfants*.

Adolescents, disasters and other failed escapes

If *Au revoir les enfants* is taken as a complex attempt to reintegrate a historical trauma into the present, what does this perspective mean for our understanding of Malle's previous work? As I raised in the previous chapter of this book, films like *Atlantic City USA* work entirely around discussions of the difficulties of recovering from

traumatic events. Likewise there seems to be a more general propensity in Mallean films for repression, with each project rewriting
the legacy of the previous film. To begin to offer a more developed
answer to my question I want to analyse two different, earlier Malle
films from the 1960s to assess whether they already point to
repressions, allusions or screened recollections of January 1944. Let
us concentrate on *Zazie dans le métro* and *Le Voleur*, one a well-known
Malle film, the other a less popular work from his canon. These early
films, both pre-May '68 pictures, are powerful examples of how
Mallean cinema does quickly seem almost saturated with meanings
that originate in the historical episode only later fully revealed in *Au
revoir les enfants*. However, in pursuing this discussion I want also to
show how this type of *post-facto* psychoanalytic explanation of Malle's
career runs into difficulties. In short, paradoxically, the clarity that
this type of psychoanalytic reading offers is ultimately reductive. It is
too heavy an analytical device for a director who so prized ambiguity,
multiple explanations and libertarianism.

Malle has regarded *Zazie dans le métro* as the beginning point in
his journey to making *Au revoir les enfants*. Talking about the film to
Philip French, he implied the connections: 'I suppose with *Zazie* I
discovered what has possibly been a major theme in films like
Lacombe Lucien, *Le Souffle au cœur*, *Au revoir les enfants*, and certainly
Pretty Baby too – at the centre of the film is a child, an adolescent who
is exposed to the hypocrisy and corruption of the world of grown-ups.
Its very obvious to me now but I'm not sure I knew it at the time'
(Malle and French 1993: 28). This statement highlights just the type
of links a psychoanalytic reading of the work would exploit. A scan
through the filmography provides numerous depictions of Mallean
children and their damaged lives, their losses of innocence. In short,
Malle's work displays an almost obsessive preoccupation with
teenagers, their youth and corruption. On a certain level, much of
Malle's work seems to anticipate *Au revoir les enfants*.

However, despite this thematic overlap, one must also show caution
when pursuing the argument. If we acknowledge the intriguing
overlaps between Malle's own traumatic youth and his later propensity to make films like *Zazie*, we must also be alert to the fact that
Malle's choices were not only determined by such psychological
factors. In the case of *Zazie dans le métro*, there were numerous
reasons why Malle chose to film this story of a young girl's loss of

innocence, her ageing, that are completely unrelated to unconscious deliberations on January 1944. Malle was attracted to novelist Raymond Queneau's surrealist background, similarly, he saw the work as a way to be more experimental in his film-making. Malle's decision to adapt a recent hit novel was also a reasonable economic proposition. *Zazie* was a project that the still relatively young production company NEF could handle with some confidence. None of the above factors suggest a profound psychological process at work. What they do remind us of is the fact that one should not too quickly reread all of Malle's work in the light of the revelations of *Au revoir les enfants*.

Nonetheless, the final scenes from *Zazie dans le métro* point to a second recurrent trope in Mallean film that can be interpreted as an artistic attempt to grapple with a childhood trauma. As Zazie's Parisian vacation is ending, the family-run café-bar where she and her relatives are staying is suddenly disrupted by a bizarre black-shirted tyrant and his aggressive supporters. Zazie, the young teenager on her first trip to the capital city, witnesses the world literally falling apart before her very eyes. Innovatively, Malle's café set is smashed to pieces by the gang and beneath the 1960s chrome and mirrors a more traditional bar room, from a different era, is revealed. Zazie sits at her table as the mayhem ensues. The Paris of the present violently collapses into the Paris of the past. Notwithstanding the broadly comedic register of the work, it seems to me that this passage from *Zazie* relates to Malle's own experience. The filming of the scene, the proximity of its content to Malle's own experience of violent fascist disruption, form strong grounds to suggest that we are watching a tentative attempt to address a buried shame, to forget by turning tragedy into comedy.

Malle's camera was regularly attracted to societies or social groups that appear to be in collapse. Malle's quasi-fascist anti-heroes of *Ascenseur pour l'échafaud* and *Le Feu follet* are exemplary. They too represent an interest in an ideology that was in turmoil, if not complete collapse. Malle's choice to work on these figures, these defeated individuals without political hope in a post-war Europe, is indicative of a fascination with disruption and failure. Similarly, Malle's documentary work offers rich illustrations of the wider tendency. Malle's final remarks from the *L'Inde fantôme* series capture a similar emphasis on despair and violent rupture. The director explains:

> In India we have been fascinated by another kind of existence –
> another kind of looking at things, for which we all feel a yearning – as
> if for some secret lost forever. Yet we feel all along that this traditional
> India was going to pass away to be crushed by civilisation ... The
> modern world brings with it the exploitation of man by his brother.
> (1968: Episode 7: *Bombay – the Future of India*)

The black-shirts shattering of the café in *Zazie*, the almost patho-
logical recurrence of figures of failure, the above assessment of India,
these examples are indicative of a man whose early life experiences
drew him to such bleak subjects. So, generally speaking, it is safe to
say that Malle did experience a sudden trauma (the Nazi raid) in his
youth and he did choose to film comparable but different experiences
across a wide range of different contexts and settings. On the other
hand, as I have discussed in Chapter 1 of this book, one must also
recall that a majority of Malle's filmic decisions can be seen to be
more related to the cultural trends of their own day than to the
experience of 1944; for instance, the similar attractions to pessimism
and disaster found in the work of the Hussard novelist, Nimier or in
F. Scott Fitzgerald's 'Babylon Revisited', a short story Malle evoked in
Le Feu follet. It is therefore too simplistic to see Malle only as a
director who was exclusively driven by his demons. Malle was surely
just as shaped by the wider social environment: his family, his education, the success of the New Wave, the Hussard literary movement
and the spirit of May '68 ... as he was working under the shadow of
1944.

The subject of *Le Voleur* is the compulsive thief, Georges Randal.
Although no direct references are made to Malle's experience of the
occupation, it is a relevant work to our discussion for several reasons.
The plot and thematic ground of *Le Voleur* hinge around an account of
a trauma and its long-term psychological consequences. At the beginning of the film Malle depicts Randal enjoying an idyllic childhood, he
is a happy-go-lucky fellow who is passionately in love with his
stepfather's daughter, Charlotte. Suddenly, Malle's narrative crushes
this optimism. In a vertiginous passage, which gains in dramatic
power by being telescoped into just a few minutes, we witness Randal
returning home from national service. He discovers that Charlotte is
engaged to be married to a different suitor and that his stepfather has
squandered, or indirectly stolen his substantial inheritance. As a
direct consequence of these disasters Malle shows how Randal is

thrown into a life of crime. Towards the conclusion of *Le Voleur*, Randal reflects on his lifestory:

> Charlotte: Is it stronger than you? [stealing]
> Randal: Stronger than anything. The first time, at Montareuil's house I didn't realise it ... but when I broke into that bureau and I saw the jewels glitter in the darkness ... I felt their weight in my hand. I had done that to vindicate myself against your father as an act of defiance. Suddenly I achieved happiness ... I felt alive ... I was fulfilled ... joy ... At night in an unknown house, while everything sleeps and I arrive ... and with that disembowelled thing ... it's as though I was born into the world.
> Charlotte: And afterwards?
> Randal: Afterwards? I feel ashamed ... I am nothing once more. I wait for the next time. (Malle, Carrière and Boulanger 1967 [printed and translated typescript, BFI collection]: 39)

Malle presents Randal's addiction to stealing as his psychological response to a childhood trauma: the moment when Randal's dream's were cruelly dashed by his stepfather. Obsessive re-enactments are the addictive driving force of Randal's life and self-identity. So, in filming *Le Voleur* Malle captures the emotions of an individual who is trapped in a perpetual struggle with a founding, but highly negative, experience, a kind of rebirth. Here, Randal's fictional life and Malle's historical experience seem to collide. The two men have experienced major turmoils in their youth: one plays them out through crime, the other through his life as a director, repeating the scopic scene of betrayal (guilt) with every look through the camera lens.

The narrative structure and visual composition of *Le Voleur* bring an additional dimension into play. *Le Voleur* begins with an extended burglary in which Randal starts to violate a bourgeois mansion. The manner in which Malle films the sequence is I think especially telling. Impressive sets of heavy dark furniture, and gold and black cabinets loom out of the night. In their midst Randal pursues his task with an unremitting violence, smashing anything that stands between him and his treasure/pleasure. The psychological depth of the action is underlined by Malle's use of lighting, with Randal often being surrounded by darkness, his white cuffs and collars gleaming out of the gloom. In fact, Malle's film portrays the burglary as a kind of passionate struggle to escape, to break out, rather than the empirically more accurate aim of breaking in. Finally, Randal does escape, he leaves the building and casually strolls to a village railway station to return to Paris. However, the clear inference of these scenes is that Randal is anything but a free man. In the melancholy light of a cold winter dawn, similar in some ways to the colours used years later in *Au revoir les enfants*, it is plain to see that Randal will commit new burglaries. Time and again he will have to repeat his initial reaction to his stepfather's betrayal. Notably, the scene captures Malle's wider preoccupation with the idea of failed escapes. This thematic preference began right at the beginning of the career with *Ascenseur pour l'échafaud*, it is hinted at throughout *Le Feu follet* and only concludes with the doomed lovers that are the subject of *Damage*. With this type of repeated psycho-narrative on show in Malle's fiction it is tempting to interpret his work as a repeated dramatic struggle for freedom from guilt, freedom from trauma. This struggle is shown to be an impossible battle and by implication the childhood trauma becomes a deadweight on the director's imagination.

One can reread Malle as a director whose work does strongly reflect a gradual working towards the completion of *Au revoir les enfants*. Malle's is a career in which one can discern the long shadow of 1944. However, as I have already also explained there are so many other cultural, social, artistic and political factors that cast light on Malle's films and that have little if any relationship to the psychological or traumatic. As Pierre Billard's biography frequently implies, Malle's decisions to choose a project to film were subject to numerous external factors: factors of production, the availability of actors and actresses, literary influence, and so on. Indeed, as I have shown there are numerous possible interpretations of Mallean film available today, and his films resist interpretation through a deliberate ambiguity. Furthermore, as Thomas Elsaesser wisely highlights in relation to this theoretical ground there is a further major complexity. If the trauma requires complete repression/forgetting then our only evidence for it would be silence and absence, a complete forgetting. Elsaesser explains the logic: 'If trauma is experienced through its forgetting, its repeated forgetting, then paradoxically, one of the signs of the presence of trauma is the absence of all signs of it' (2001: 199). Film – especially Mallean film – works on the basis of the opposite of this situation. Paradoxically, it reverberates with disturbed adolescents, social worlds at their breaking points and so many failed escapes.

Rereading the Philip French interviews it is clear that Malle favoured a trauma theory reinterpretation of his work. Here was a version of his life and work that he was most happy for the public to use. We need not dispute that point of view, it accurately illustrates Malle's own thinking of the late 1980s and early 1990s. However, we should also be aware that the pose does not provide a definitive response to the artist's work.

Au revoir les enfants: a political reinterpretation

I want to return now to *Au revoir les enfants* and to offer a more politicised discussion, in so doing to demonstrate that there are other enriching ways of interpreting Malle's film. The work is a significant contribution to the portrayal of the Holocaust in French cinema. It also represents Malle's most persuasive libertarian confrontation with authority.

Notwithstanding the relative attractions of applying psychoanalytic theory to the work, or the theme of guilt, what does Malle have to say about the Holocaust in *Au revoir les enfants*? Saul Friedländer has suggested that most representations of Nazi genocide will work around a basic characterisation pattern based on the portrayal of persecutors, bystanders and victims (1988: 66–77). Malle's work conforms to Friedländer's basic character types but it also projects new and resonant meanings on to them. Clearly, Malle's work has its victims: Bonnet, Négus and Dupré. Similarly, Malle sharply defines the persecutors as the Nazis, notably the Gestapo officer, Müller, who leads the raid in the film. Likewise, the brutally anti-Semitic French militia men that Malle also presents in his film fall into the same category. However, the psychoanalytic vector through which Malle casts his surrogate, Quentin, disturbs and problematises the figure of the bystander. On the one hand, the introduction of Quentin's guilty looks, his final act of betrayal, positions this version of the bystander nearer to the role traditionally occupied by the persecutors in other Holocaust narratives. As Higgins correctly identified, in the final scenes of the film Quentin practically becomes a collaborator when he indirectly betrays Bonnet (1992: 207). Here, then, is a representation of the bystander that is relatively common in most liberal depictions of the Holocaust. It is the variant that presents the bystander as complicit to the act of persecution. As Friedländer remarks of this variation: 'It is the representation most of us have of what has happened' (1988: 69). Similarly, as Friedländer also explains, variations on the rhetorical pattern are found across genres: 'the narrative implies global historical responsibility ... It has found manifold modes of expression, over the last forty years, in the news media, literature and film' (Friedländer 1988: 69).

However, Malle's bystander is also filmed from a different perspective. Notably, through the film's emphasis on Malle's framing memory of these events (I'll remember that morning') we see Quentin as another kind of child victim, and also a traumatised adult remembering a life-long guilt. Malle suggests that he/Quentin have lived under the memory of a tormented past, rather like a Holocaust survivor. With this emphasis Malle allows his autobiographical figuration of the bystander to slide very close to the category of victim. In his emphasis on the ambiguity of the bystander, Malle is creating an original discourse on the Holocaust. Now, it is important to be precise: the portrayal does not represent a version of the right-wing revisionism along the lines of the German pulp fiction (the novels of Konsalik) that cast Nazi perpetrators as 'victims' of new 'Stalinist persecutors'. Instead, in Malle's problematising of the bystander the basic categories of persecutor and victim are left unchallenged. They are not Malle's central concern. What Malle is saying in this powerful film is that the role of the bystander implies not only complicity in the Holocaust. The very same position also encompasses the fear and terror of being a victim, the shared sense of guilt of surviving the disaster.

I suppose, given what we know about Malle's propensity for ambiguity, the above handling of the bystander is a predictable strategy. Nevertheless, unlike the oscillating portrayals of fascism or child prostitution found in *Lacombe Lucien* or *Pretty Baby* (that are discussed in Chapter 4), the ambiguous Mallean bystander achieves a level of poetic truth. Malle's representational strategy in *Au revoir les enfants* captures a genuine tension in the experience of bystanders. His film functions around the blurred boundaries of what it means to have witnessed, suffered, but not actually to have been the subject of genocidal persecution. This portrayal invites audiences to think beyond Nazis and Jews and to interrogate the role of everyone else living in Europe in that period of genocide. In this way Malle's film charts new gradations and subtleties in the historical experience of the Holocaust.

Malle's interpretation of the bystander is also important because it inevitably comes closest to the position of contemporary cinemagoers who are too young to have experienced the Holocaust itself. Most viewers born after 1945 cannot literally share the space of persecutor (Nazi) or victims (Jew, resistant or other targeted minority group such as Roma Sinti, homosexuals or lesbians). Therefore, the temporal distance from the events of the Holocaust place many of us closer to the role of the bystander: Malle/Quentin. So post-Holocaust generations strangely resemble Malle's subject. Like Julien Quentin in his classroom we are unable to do anything to alter the course of European history in the 1940s. In that sense we resemble the powerless victim side of Malle's bystander. On the other hand, this paralysis is equally suggestive of the shared guilt of former persecutors. These interactions between Malle, *Au revoir les enfants*, and its late 1980s audience combine to make the film a unique representation of the 1940s.

Even the best readers of Malle – Golsan (2001), Higgins (1992) or Kedward (2000) – have overlooked the profound attack on authority that Malle pursued in *Au revoir les enfants*. While many previous Malle films critique bourgeois society, sexual hypocrisies or social inequities, it is arguably in *Au revoir les enfants* that the most subtle and controlled version of Malle's dignified anger with society is articulated. Importantly, in this film Malle presents two key speeches on the idea of duty and good behaviour. Malle's handling of these statements show a continued hatred for order, authority and the pain that these values bring.

Caught in the emotional drama of a first viewing of *Au revoir les enfants* it is easy to disregard the final words Malle attributes to the Nazi offcier, Müller. While the children take part in the humiliating role call, a German soldier interrupts his superior to report that he has found three young women in the chapel. The soldier stands by them looking at his officer, Müller. Subsequently, one of the women cries out: 'On était venues se confesser' ('We came to confession'). Pompously, Müller states, to the women, to the schoolboys and also to the audience of the film: 'Ce soldat a fait son devoir. Il avait l'ordre de ne laisser sortir personne. La discipline est la force du soldat allemand. Ce qui vous manque, à vous Français, c'est la discipline.

Nous ne sommes pas vos ennemis. Vous devez nous aider à débarrasser la France des étrangers, des juifs' (Malle 1987: 131).[4]

Malle's decision to include this speech and the scene that frames it is important. Certainly, it asserts the subtle historical comment that not only German Gestapo officers but also ordinary soldiers were part of the Holocaust (a point of some historical controversy in West Germany and Austria by the late 1980s). However, more significantly, in the context of the politics of Malle's wider filmography, the scene also offers a decisive confrontation with the value system that Malle's libertarian imagination detested: discipline, duty, order, authority. The implication Malle makes here is that the martial values that Müller praises – discipline, the unthinking respect for authority (for that is what following orders ultimately represents) – are the very qualities that underpin genocide. This is an unusually *unambiguous* rhetorical move on Malle's part. Nevertheless, it asserts a continuity in his work in that it clarifies his anti-authoritarianism of the 1970s by weaving it into his most decisive cinematic intervention.

Müller is not the only authority figure dissected by Malle in *Au revoir les enfants*. Indeed, Malle generally shows the Petit Collège des Carmes as a hierarchical institution in which Catholic morality is the controlling ideological force. Importantly, also towards the end of the film, but prior to the Nazi officer's speech, Malle allows Père Jean (based on Jacques) to pronounce a statement that summarises a second political and moral outlook. Jean presents a sermon and the words that he employs are radical. He proclaims: 'Mes enfants, nous vivons des temps de discorde et de haine. Le mensonge est tout puissant, les chrétiens s'entre-tuent, ceux qui devraient nous guider nous trahissent. Plus que jamais, nous devons nous garder de l'égoïsme et de l'indifférence' (Malle 1987: 86).[5] He continues by citing the classic parable of the rich man and the eye of the needle. However, the sermon is concluded with a very Mallean sounding assertion on the perils of judgement. Jean declares: 'Saint Paul nous dit dans l'Epître d'aujourd'hui: "Frères, ne vous prenez pas pour des

4 'That soldier is doing his duty. He had orders not to let anyone leave. Discipline is the strength of the German soldier. That's what you French lack: discipline. We are not your enemies. You have to help us rid France of foreigners, of Jews.'

5 'My children we are living in times of discord and hatred. The lie is all powerful; Christians are killing other Christians; those who should lead us, betray us. More than ever we have to guard against egoism and indifference.'

sages. Ne rendez à personne le mal pour le mal. Si ton ennemi a faim, donne-lui à manger. S'il a soif, donne-lui à boire." Nous allons prier pour ceux qui souffrent, ceux qui ont faim, ceux que l'on persécute. Nous allons prier pour les victimes, et aussi pour les bourreaux' (Malle 1987: 87–8).[6] Clearly, on one level of interpretation, here is a statement that Malle introduces to his film in order to agree with it broadly. Jean's sentiments correspond to Malle's own cinematic and moral preference to try to understand all experiences, to be careful not to judge or condemn too quickly. Similarly, Jean's speech functions as a symbolic counterpoint to the value system that is later presented though the words of the Nazi, Müller.

Significantly, Malle does not leave the meaning of the Priest's speech as an unproblematic lesson, a simple moral to live by. Instead, Malle shows that it is the same Priest's later breech of his values that incites the Nazi raid. Only minutes later in the film Joseph, a crippled teenager who works in the school kitchens, is found engaged in black-market dealing. The pupils found to be involved in the black market are left with only a minor punishment. Conversely, the Priests send the kitchen-hand Joseph away from the school. He is expelled from the community that he had been a part of. So, at precisely the moment in Malle's film when Jean is offered an opportunity to 'not return harm for harm' he fails to follow the lesson of Saint Paul that he had cited in his own oration. Joseph is wrongly punished, he is treated with egoism and indifference. Subsequently, Malle's narrative informs us that because of this decision Joseph finds solace in collaboration with the Nazi authorities. Indirectly, it is the failure of Père Jean to live up to his own worldview that precipitates the tragic conclusion to the film. I think what Malle is saying through Jean's speech, and the subsequent plot developments that follow from it, is that there is an intrinsic danger to any moral pronouncement, however worthy it might sound. The words of Père Jean's speech offer a value system that Malle supports. However, when tested in practice, Malle implies that the words of the speech are actually meaningless and deceptive froth. So for Malle even a moral code that he can sympathise with is

6 'Saint Paul tells us "Brethren, do not think you are all knowing. Do not return harm for harm. If your enemy is hungry, give him food. If he is thirsty, give him drink." We shall pray for those who are suffering, those who are hungry, those who are being persecuted. We shall pray for the victims and for their tormentors.'

inevitably tainted. Malle's film implies that a priest cannot instruct forgiveness any more than a uniformed Nazi can order discipline. Both are politically damaged in advance because of the speaking positions from which they emanate. In *Au revoir les enfants* we are shown the consequence of hierarchy and authority. The words of the Nazi officer lead to barbarity, the words of the priest to hypocrisy and tragedy. Both men and the sites of power they hold are utterly condemned.

Malle also uses *Au revoir les enfants* to underline two positive models of social learning and interaction. Once more abandoning his former preference for ambiguity and resolute avoidance of political judgement, Malle's film implies that art is perhaps the only road to happiness and social freedom. Thus, Malle cleverly shows cinema and jazz music as providing ways of creating friendships that are not based on authority or elitism. There are two touching and relevant scenes from the film where Malle outlines these possibilities. First, there is the role played by the cinema in *Au revoir les enfants*. To make his point Malle introduces a 'film within his film'. A little improbably, the priests organise a showing of Charlie Chaplin's *The Immigrant*. The whole school is gathered to watch the film and in front of the flickering images of Chaplin they look more like a strong and rounded community than at any other time. In a period of genocidal warfare a passage of respite has been found through the cinema. Malle's handling of the scene implies a kind of new-found social egalitarianism. The children, Gentiles and Jews, the monks, and Joseph (the future victim of Catholic hypocrisy), are presented by Malle as a united group.

Malle later implies that jazz music can bring a similar moment of relief and social freedom. Thus, Malle films Quentin and Bonnet together by the school piano. An air raid siren screams out but the boys stay together. Bonnet, who is the better pianist, kindly teaches Quentin a series of simple notes. Next, Malle portrays the two boys playing an impromptu two-handed boogie-woogie number together. Their combined efforts produce an exuberant tune. Now, Malle's dominant representational handling of the relationship, the voyeuristic looking from Quentin to Bonnet, is briefly abandoned in favour of a far more egalitarian perspective. Standing side by side the boys laugh and play together. Malle suggests that all racial boundaries are now temporarily broken down, and perhaps also that the two sides of this 'double' are united in a single aural experience. To emphasise the point, it is only following this scene that Malle indicates that Julien and Bonnet's conversations have become relaxed and terrifyingly honest. Malle portrays Julien trying to understand humanely Bonnet's terrible plight. Calmly, Quentin asks: 'tu as peur' and Bonnet replies: 'Tout le temps' ('Are you afraid?'; 'All the time') (Malle 1987: 115).

In *Au revoir les enfants* cinema and jazz offer transcendence and hope. More importantly Malle shows these art forms as not being dependent on any kind of system of authority, power or moral regulation. *Au revoir les enfants* contains one of Malle's clearest and most attractive political excursions. Life has choices and in this work Malle suggests that authority leads to corrupt, if not evil, actions. By way of contrast, the life of the community and Quentin and Bonnet are shown to be far better served by the popular arts of cinema and jazz. The implicit comparison Malle pursues represents a refreshing and different kind of Mallean politics to that found in his films from the 1950s or 1970s. With the lightest of touches a critique of power is offered. Similarly, a loose, perhaps utopian, alternative socio-political position is sketched out by way of the glorification of the arts. It is unusual to witness Malle offering a positive quasi-political assertion such as this. It is less surprising that when such a discourse is presented that it should valorise cinema itself.

Conclusion

Malle's cinema quickly lends itself to psychoanalytic interpretation. Despite some of the reservations I have expressed, Lynn Higgins' application of the idea of the primal scene/trauma theory to *Au revoir les enfants* is a fruitful line of enquiry. Numerous Louis Malle films evoke the events of January 1944 and thus also anticipate *Au revoir les enfants*.

It is tempting and plausible to present Malle as a director haunted by history, his chidlhood trauma played out throughout his career. This version of Mallean cinema was what Malle was most happy with in public discussions of his work at the end of his life. Malle was clearly happy with the idea that *Au revoir les enfants* resolved a trauma, that it revealed a repressed episode, and offered unified thematic ground through which to look back on his life and films. The interpretation functions as a kind of negative foundation myth explaining everything from *Ascenseur pour l'échafaud* to *Damage*. The interpretation also has its functional side, providing Mallean cinema with a defining leitmotif that was very much in tune with the commemorative mood of the later 1980s, the bicentenary of the revolution, the fortieth and fiftieth commemorations of the Second World War. However, to borrow from Thomas Elsaesser's recent theorising on trauma and film we must also recall that this is ultimately just one interpretative mode based on the discovery of referentiality across Malle's films (2001: 201). Like most interpretations then it is subject to its own ambiguities, weaknesses and concealments. While films like *Zazie dans le métro* or *Le Voleur* seem to exemplify a cinema of trauma and repression, so much of Malle's work also falls outside the terms of this perspective that it becomes reductive to force Malle in to a single psychologically driven mode of interpretation.

Thinking about Louis Malle in the light of Freud's notion of the uncanny is a different critical opportunity to the trauma-repression approach to his work. Malle's treatments of 'the double' or the 'evil eye', bring new insights to *Au revoir les enfants* and Malle's wider work. This is a second look at the director's work that deserves greater attention. Indeed, one gains much through reference to the question of the 'double' when returning to Malle's rhetoric of ambiguity, for it too hinges on uncanny duplications and repetitions.

Finally, there is a powerful political subtext at work in *Au revoir les enfants* which makes the film a far more important contribution to cinema than has been sometimes surmised by other critics of Malle. *Au revoir les enfants* reminds us of the dynamics and consequences of social authority and political power. In counterpoint, Malle also explores how film and music provide ways of communicating, community-building and enhancing social experience. In our own times of academic, intellectual and political conformity, every opportunity to reassert a political reading of *Au revoir les enfants* is surely at a premium.

References

Braunschweig, Maryvonne and Bernard Gidel (1989) *Les Déportés d'Avon. Enquête autour du film de Louis Malle, Au revoir les enfants* (Paris: La Découverte).

Carrouges, Michel (1988) *Le Père Jacques* (Paris: Cerf).

Elsaesser, Thomas (2001) 'Postmodernism as Mourning-Work', *Screen* 42.2: 193–201.

Fogelman, Eva (1993) 'The Psychology Behind Being a Hidden Child', in Jane Marks (ed.) *The Hidden Children* (London: Piatkus): 292–307.

Frappat, Hélène 'Le fantôme de la liberté', *Cahiers du cinéma*, 571 (2002): 76–7.

Freud, Sigmund [1919] (1985) 'The Uncanny', in *Sigmund Freud: Art and Literature*, vol. 14, *Penguin Freud Library* (London: Pengiun): 339–76.

Friedländer, Saul (1988) 'Historical Writing and the Memory of the Holocaust', in Berel Lang (ed.) *Writing and the Holocaust* (New York: Holmes and Meier): 66–77.

Golsan, Richard J. (2000) *Vichy's Afterlife: History and Counterhistory in Postwar France* (Lincoln and London: University of Nebraska Press).

Guérin, Alain (2000) *Chronique de la Résistance* (Paris: Omnibus).

Higgins, Lynn (1992) 'If Looks Could Kill: Louis Malle's Portraits of Collaboration', in Richard Golsan (ed.), *Fascism, Aesthetics and Culture* (Hanover: University Press of New England): 198–212.

Kedward, Roderick (2000) '*Lacombe Lucien* and the Anti-Carnival of Collaboration', in Susan Hayward and Ginette Vincendeau (eds), *French Film: Texts and Contexts* (London: Routledge): 227–39.

Klarsfeld, Serge and Claude Bochurberg (1997) *Entretiens avec Serge Klarsfeld* (Paris: Stock).

Malle, Louis, Daniel Boulanger and Jean-Claude Carrière (1967) *Le Voleur* (London: BFI [unpublished script to the film, reneotyped in English translation]).

Malle, Louis (1978) *Louis Malle par Louis Malle* (Paris: L'Athanor).

Malle, Louis (1987) *Au revoir les enfants* (Paris: Gallimard).

Royle, Nicholas (2003) *The Uncanny* (Manchester: Manchester University Press).

Wilson, Emma (1999) *French Cinema since 1950* (New York: Rowman and Littlefield Publications).

6

Conclusion

In dissecting a lifetime of ambiguity this book has shown that there are few critical certainties when it comes to Malle. This is the most fascinating quality of Mallean cinema. It is the hook that makes one want to continue learning about the man and his work. Nevertheless, where do the contradictions end? With what kind of final freeze-frame images can one leave the director and his films?

Points of stability and continuity have been established. Malle's childhood experience of January 1944, the founding trauma, its working-through in the eventual completion of *Au revoir les enfants*, provides one coherent and important way to debate the director and his work. As Malle frequently implied towards the end of his life his cinema can be interpreted as a long artistic struggle with the shattering events of a Saturday morning in the winter of 1944. Nevertheless, legitimate doubts remain as to the efficacy of this approach when reductively applied to Mallean film. As I suggested in the previous chapter this line of argument, however attractive, almost over-explains Malle's career. Much is gained but much is also lost with this interpretation, not least the value of different psychoanalytic modes of enquiry like Freud's 'uncanny double'.

Beyond the psychoanalytic, as I showed in Chapter 1 there is Malle 'the ambiguous director of and for his times'. There is Malle the 1950s playboy celebrity, the *soixante-huitard* activist, the Frenchman at home in New York and Hollywood. Similarly, it is essential to underline Malle's status as the professional *cinéaste*, producer, documentarist and artist of the moving image. In other words, there are great technical achievements here, even if they are tainted with social or political views we might disagree with. Malle's preferred form of film-making was a unique aesthetic synthesis. Classical realism, surrealism and *cinéma direct* continue to be a powerful combination that defies simplistic aesthetic classification.

Two potentially less reassuring outlooks on Mallean film have been presented when exploring the director's work from the late 1950s and the 1970s. Intentionally or otherwise, films like *Ascenseur pour l'échafaud*, *Les Amants* and *Le Feu follet* popularised sensibilities that were commonly held in the right-wing conservative counterculture. Malle was not alone in adopting this perspective and bringing it to French cinema screens. His cinema of active pessimism continues to challenge bourgeois complacency, it includes an unusual but also incisive critique of post-war France. One does not have to unthinkingly agree with Malle's outlook to appreciate its rhetorical force. Furthermore, with *Le Souffle au cœur* Malle drifted away from this discourse towards a different kind of film-making. With the completion of that film a phase in Malle's life and work was closed.

The libertarian memorial activist of the 1970s is as troubling a figure as the 'Hussard' pessimist. *Lacombe Lucien* is a masterwork of the visual rhetoric of ambiguity. However, the central representational strategy Malle used was an especially disturbing choice. The replication of a comparable rhetorical approach to the theme of child prostitution in *Pretty Baby* marks the scope of Malle's radicalism. This film captures the risks Malle ran and sometimes did not escape from when filming controversial material without also offering even a hint of a firm ethical position. Nonetheless, Malle was true to his declared fidelity to his terrifying childhood experience of Nazi-occupied France. In filming *Au revoir les enfants* he systematically asserted a defence of artistic liberty against unthinking authoritarianism. Today, that kind of non-conformism is refreshingly welcome. Malle's memorial activism is at a new premium because it invites audiences to think for themselves.

Mallean film was also a journey of repeated reinvention. Film after film recoded public perceptions of the director and his previous work. In this way the same director who collaborated with Nimier on *Ascenseur pour l'échafaud* was able to later work on *Le Souffle au cœur*, or to offer *Pretty Baby* just ten years before making *Au revoir les enfants*. Reinvention and the repression of past projects was the way to smooth over perplexing contradictions. By all accounts the strategy was highly successful. This process is a further defining characteristic of Malle's cinema. Indeed, one could argue that Malle's films from the 1970s tended to revise his work from the 1950s. In turn the films from the 1980s like *Au revoir les enfants* and *Milou en mai* reshaped the status of those interim pictures. For this reason it is essential for students of Malle to glide confidently forward and backwards through the oeuvre. Malle's work often asks us to try to forget linear versions of historical progress in favour of more circular readings.

These are the central elements of Mallean cinema that I have analysed in this study. To assert one version of Malle over another would be cavalier and futile. To erect one monumental interpretation of his cinema over another is a foolhardy venture as doomed to failure as Julien Tavernier's original *crime passionnel* committed in *Ascenseur pour l'échafaud*. For such a critical act denies ambiguity to a director whose work relied so greatly on that still troubling and captivating quality.

Filmography

Le Monde du Silence (1956) (UK/USA: ***The Silent World***) 86 min., col.

Directed: Jacques-Yves Cousteau
Co-directed: Louis Malle
Production: Société Filmad and Requins Associés
Photography: Edmond Séchan
Editing: Georges Alépée
Sound: Yves Baudrier
Commentary: James Dugan

Ascenseur pour l'échafaud (1957) (UK: ***Lift to the Scaffold***; USA: ***Elevator to the Gallows***) 90 min., b/w.

Production: Jean Thuiller/Nouvelles Editions de Films (henceforth NEF)
Screenplay: Louis Malle and Roger Nimier from the novel by Noel Calef
Photography: Henri Decae
Editing: Léonide Azar
Sound: Raymond Gauguier, with music from Miles Davis
Principal actors: Maurice Ronet (Julien Tavernier), Jeanne Moreau
  (Florence Carala), Georges Poujoly (Louis); and Yori Bertin (Véronique)

Les Amants (1958) (UK/USA: ***The Lovers***) 88 min., b/w.

Production: NEF
Screenplay: Louis Malle and Louise de Vilmorin
Photography: Henri Decae
Editing: Léonide Azar
Sound: Pierre Bertrand
Principal actors: Jeanne Moreau (Jeanne Tournier), Alain Cuny (Henri
  Tournier) and Jean-Marc Bory (Bernard Dubois-Lambert)

Zazie dans le métro (1960) (UK/USA: ***Zazie***) 92 min., col.

Production: NEF
Screenplay: Louis Malle and Jean-Paul Rappeneau from the novel by
  Raymond Queneau
Photography: Henri Raichi
Editing: Kenout Peltier
Sound: André Hervé
Principal actors: Catherine Demongeot (Zazie), Philippe Noiret (Uncle
  Gabriel), Carla Marlier (Aunt Albertine), Vittorio Capriolli (Pedro
  Trouscaillon), Hubert Deschamps (Turandot) and Jacques Dufilho
  (Gridoux)

Vie privée (1961) (UK/USA: ***A Very Private Affair***) 103 min., col. (Dubbed
English-language version 94 min.)

Production: Fanco-Italian co-production Progefi, Cipra (France) and CCM
  (Rome)
Screenplay: Louis Malle, Jean-Paul Rappeneau and Jean Ferry
Photography: Henri Decae
Editing: Kenout Peltier
Sound: William Robert Sivel
Principal actors: Brigitte Bardot (Jill) and Marcello Mastroianni (Fabio)

Vive Le Tour (1962) (UK: ***Louis Malle's Vive Le Tour***) 18 min., col.

Production: Louis Malle
Photography: Jacques Ertaud, Ghislain Cloquet and Louis Malle
Editing: Kenout Peltier and Suzanne Baron

Le Feu follet (1963) (UK: ***A Time to Live and a Time to Die***; USA: ***The Fire
Within***) 110 min., b/w.

Production: NEF
Screenplay: Louis Malle from the novel by Pierre Drieu La Rochelle
Photography: Ghislain Cloquet
Editing: Suzanne Baron
Sound: Music by Claude Helffer
Principal actors: Maurice Ronet (Alain Leroy), Léna Sklerla (Lydia),
  Bernard Noël (Dubourg), Jeanne Moreau (Jeanne), Alexander Stewart
  (Solange) and Tony Taffin (Brancion)

Viva Maria (1965) 115 min., col.

Production: NEF, United Artists (UA) and Vides (Rome)
Screenplay: Louis Malle and Jean-Claude Carrière
Photography: Henri Decae

Editing: Kenout Peltier and Suzanne Baron

Sound: José B. Carles

Principal actors: Jeanne Moreau (Maria I) Brigitte Bardot (Maria II), Georges Hamilton (Florès) and Paulette Dubost (Mme Diogène)

Le Voleur (1967) (USA: *The Thief of Paris*) 120 min., col.

Production: NEF, United Artsists and Compania Cinematografica Montoro (Italy)

Screenplay: Louis Malle, Jean-Claude Carrière with dialogue by Daniel Boulanger after the novel by Georges Darien

Photography: Henri Decae

Editing: Henri Lanoe

Sound: André Hervé

Principal actors: Jean-Paul Belmondo (Georges Randal), Geneviève Bujold (Charlotte), Julien Guiomar (Abbé La Margelle), Christian Lude (Uncle Urbain) and Charles Denner (Cannonier)

Histoires Extraordinaires (1967) (UK: *Tales of Terror*; USA: *Spirits of the Dead* (a film in three-parts)) 121 min., col.

William Wilson directed by Louis Malle, with *Metzengerstein* directed by Roger Vadim and *Toby Dammit* directed by Federico Fellini

Production: Les Films Marceau-Cocinor (Paris) and PEA Cinematografica (Rome)

Screenplay for *William Wilson*: Louis Malle, Daniel Boulanger and Clement Biddle Wood

Photography for *William Wilson*: Tonino Delli Colli

Editing: Franco Arcalli and Suzanne Baron

Sound: Music by Diego Masson

Principal actors for *William Wilson*: Alain Delon (William Wilson) and Brigitte Bardot (Giuseppina)

Calcutta (1968) 105 min., col.

Production: NEF and Eliot Kastner

Screenplay/Narration: Louis Malle

Photography: Etienne Becker and Louis Malle

Editing: Suzanne Baron

Sound: Jean-Claude Laureux

L'Inde fantôme: réflexions sur un voyage (1968) (UK/USA: *Phantom India*) 378 min., col.

A seven-part television series. Titles from the BBC broadcasts are presented in parenthesis.

1 *La Caméra impossible. (The Impossible Camera)*
2 *Choses vues à Madras. (Things seen in Madras)*
3 *La Religion. (The Indians and the Sacred)*
4 *La Tentation du rêve. (Dreams and Reality)*
5 *Regards sur les castes. (A Look at the Castes)*
6 *Les Etrangers en Indes. (On the Fringes of Indian Society)*
7 *Bombay. (Bombay – the future of India)*

(Otherwise, for further details see *Calcutta* above)

Le Souffle au cœur (1971) (UK: *Dearest Love*; USA: *Murmur of the Heart*) 110 min., col.

Production: NEF and Marianne (Paris); Vides Cinematografica (Rome) and Franz Seitz Filmproduktion (Munich)
Screenplay: Louis Malle
Photography: Ricardo Aronovitch
Editing: Suzanne Baron
Sound: Jean-Claude Laureux and Michel Vionnet
Principal actors: Lea Massari (Clara), Benoît Ferreux (Laurent), Daniel Gélin (Clara's husband and Laurent's father), Michel Lonsdale (Père Henri) and Gila von Weitershausen (Freda)

Lacombe Lucien (1974) 137 min., col.

Production: NEF, UPF Paris, Vides Film (Rome) and Hallelujah Films (Munich)
Screenplay: Louis Malle and Patrick Modiano
Photography: Tonino Delli Colli
Editing: Suzanne Baron
Sound: Jean-Claude Laureux
Principal actors: Pierre Blaise (Lucien), Aurore Clément (France), Holger Löwenadler (M. Horn) and Thérèse Giehse (Bella Horn)

Humain, trop humain (1974) 75 min., col.

Production: NEF
Photography: Etienne Becker
Editing: Suzanne Baron
Sound: Jean-Claude Laureux

Place de la République (1974) 94 min., col.

Production: NEF
Photography: Etienne Becker
Editing: Suzanne Baron
Sound: Jean-Claude Laureux

Black Moon (1975) 100 min., col.

Production: NEF, UFP (Paris) and Vides Film (Rome)/ Claude Nedjar
Screenplay: Louis Malle
Photography: Sven Nykvisk
Editing: Suzanne Baron
Sound: Luc Perini
Principal actors: Cathryn Harrison (Lily), Thérèse Giehse (woman in the bed), Alexander Stewart (sister) and Joe Dallessandro (brother)

Close Up (1976) 26 min., col.

Production: Sigma-Antenne 2
Photography: Michel Parbot
Editing: Suzanne Baron
Sound: Music by Dominique Sanda

Pretty Baby (1978) (France: *La Petite*) 110 min., col.

Production: Paramount
Screenplay: Polly Platt
Photography: Sven Nykvist
Editing: Suzanne Baron and Suzanne Fenn
Sound: Don Johnson
Principal actors: Keith Carradine (EJ Bellocq), Susan Sarandon (Hattie), Brooke Shields (Violet), Frances Faye (Nell) and Antonio Fargas (Claude)

Atlantic City USA (1980) 105 min., col.

Production: Cine-Neighbour (Montreal) and Selta-Films Kfouri (Paris) with co-ordination of production by Vincent Malle
Screenplay: John Guare
Photography: Richard Ciupka
Editing: Suzanne Baron
Sound: Jean-Claude Laureux
Principal actors: Burt Lancaster (Lou), Susan Sarandon (Sally), Kate Reid (Grace) and Michel Piccoli (a croupier)

My Dinner with André (1981) 111 min., col.

Production: The André company
Screenplay: Wallace Shawn and André Gregory
Photography: Jeri Sopanen
Editing: Suzanne Baron
Sound: Jean-Claude Laureux
Principal actors: Wallace Shawn (Wally) and André Gregory (André)

Crackers (1983) 91 min., col.

Production: Universal
Screenplay: Jeffrey Fiskin (based on the Italian film, *I soliti ignoti* (*Persons Unknown*))
Photography: Laszlo Kovacs
Editing: Suzanne Baron
Sound: Music by Pal Chihara
Principal actors: Donald Sutherland (Westlake), Jack Warden (Garvey), Sean Penn (Dillard), Wallace Shawn (Turtle) and Christine Baranski (Maxine)

Alamo Bay (1985) 99 min., col.

Production: Tri-Star-Delphi III Productions
Screenplay: Alice Arlen based on articles published in the *New York Times* by Ross E.Milloy
Photography: Curtis Clark
Editing: James Bruce
Sound: Danny Michael
Principal actors: Amy Madigan (Glory), Ed Harris (Shang) and Ho Nguyen (Dinh)

God's Country (1986) (France: *Le Pays de dieu*) 95 min., col.

Production: PBS (Grant from the National Endowment for the Arts)
Screenplay: Narration by Louis Malle
Photography: Louis Malle
Editing: James Bruce
Sound: Jean-Claude Laureux and Keith Rouse

And the Pursuit of Happiness (1987) (France: *La Poursuite du bonheur*) 80 min., col.

Production: Pretty Mouse Films (New York)
Screenplay: Narration by Louis Malle
Photography: Louis Malle
Editing: Nancy Baker
Sound: Danny Michael

Au revoir les enfants (1987) 103 min., col.

Production: NEF and MK2 Productions (Marin Karmitz), Stella Film and
    NEF (Munich)
Screenplay: Louis Malle
Photography: Renato Berta
Editing: Emmanuelle Castro
Sound: Jean-Claude Laureux
Principal actors: Gaspard Manesse (Julien Quentin), Raphaël Fejtö (Jean
    Bonnet), Francine Racette (Mme Quentin), Philippe Morier-Genoud
    (Père Jean), François Négret (Joseph) and Peter Fitz (Müller)

Milou en Mai (1989) (UK: *Milou in May*; USA: *May Fools*) 108 min., col.

Production: NEF and TF1 Films (Paris), Ellepi Film (Rome)
Screenplay: Louis Malle and Jean-Claude Carrière
Photography: Renato Berta
Editing: Emmanuelle Castro
Sound: Jean-Claude Laureux
Principal actors: Michel Piccoli (Milou), Miou-Miou (Camille), Michel
    Duchaussoy (Georges), Harriet Walter (Lily), and Paulette Dubost
    (Milou's mother, Mme Vieuzac)

Damage (1992) (France: *Fatale*) 110 min., col.

Production: NEF and Skreba (UK)
Screenplay: David Hare from the novel by Josephine Hart
Photography: Peter Bizou
Editing: John Bloom
Sound: Jean-Claude Laureux
Principal actors: Jeremy Irons (Stephem Fleming MP), Juliette Binoche
    (Anna Barton), Miranda Richardson (Ingrid Fleming) and Rupert
    Graves (Martyn Fleming)

Vanya on 42nd Street (1994) (France: *Vanya 42ᵉ rue*) 120 min., col.

Production: Laura Pels Productions, Mayfair entertainment in association
    with Channel 4 Films
Screenplay: David Mamet based on Anton Chekhov's *Uncle Vanya*
Photography: Declan Quinn
Editing: Nancy Baker
Sound: Tod A. Maitland, Joel Holland and music by Joshua Redmond
Principal actors: Wallace Shawn (Vanya), Julianne Moore (Yelena) André
    Gregory (André Gregory), Georges Gaynes (Serebryakov), Brooke
    Smith (Sonya) and Larry Pine (Astrov)

Select bibliography

See also the References sections at the end of each chapter.

Autobiographical writings and major interviews

Louis Malle par Louis Malle – avec la participation de Jacques Mallécot, Paris, Editions de l'Athanor, 1978. A short autobiographical reflection by Malle on his life and work. This fascinating book also includes 'Une filmographie imaginaire' of work that Malle would have wished to film but did not manage to realise; Malle's travel writing on Algeria and India, as well as an interview with Susan Sontag devoted to *Black Moon*. It is essential reading for any one wishing to pursue further research.

Malle on Malle, edited by Philip French, London, Faber & Faber, 1993. Despite the similarity of its title to the earlier French publication this book is not a translation of Malle's first autobiographical writings. Instead, it contains a collection of interviews conducted between Malle and the British film critic, Philip French. The first edition of the title concludes with discussion of *Damage*. Later editions include an additional chapter devoted to Malle's final film, *Vanya on 42nd Street*.

Malle, Louis, 1974 'Le cinéma français et le star-system', *Le Film Français*, 8 February, 4–6. Malle expresses his dislike for the French star-system in a leading trade journal. Three years later he would leave Paris to work on *Pretty Baby* in the United States.

Malle, Louis, 1979 'Creating a Reality that Doesn't Exist: An Interview with Louis Malle', *Literature/Film Quarterly* 7.2: 86–98. A helpful interview to better understand Malle's preoccupations in the late 1970s. It was published in the United States just after the completion of *Pretty Baby*.

Malle spends a considerable amount of time discussing that film and its controversial subject matter.

'*Louis Malle*', in C. Devarrieux and M.-C. De Navacelle, *Cinéma du réel*, Paris: Autrement, 1988: 22–31. A definitive statement by Malle on his conception of *cinéma direct* documentary film-making. Important reading for anyone interested in this aspect of his career.

Malle, Louis and Marc Dambre, 1989 'Entretien exclusif avec Louis Malle', *Cahiers des amis de Roger Nimier*. 5–17. A frank discussion between Malle and the Parisian literary scholar Marc Dambre. Dambre is the author of the definitive biography of Roger Nimier. His discussions with Malle focus on this subject.

'Louis Malle on *Au revoir les enfants*', *Projections*, 9, 1999: 33–51. A translation of Malle's original interview in the French review *Positif*. It provides a useful snapshot of Malle's public persona in the late 1980s. In particular the interview covers Malle's memories of the 1940s as well as his later American career.

Critical studies and essays devoted to Malle's life and work

Arnold, Frank *et al.* (eds) *Louis Malle*, Munich and Vienna: Carl Hanser Verlag, 1985. A collection of essays and interviews devoted to Malle and his work. It remains available only in the original German edition and covers Mallean film up to and including *Alamo Bay* (1985).

Billard, P., *Louis Malle. Le Rebelle solitaire*, Paris, Plon, 2003. The first major biographical study to be published on the director since his death. The work is an impressive survey of Malle's life and times and is filled with thought-provoking material. Billard draws on previously privately held documentation, now part of an archive devoted to the director (BIFI, Paris). The general tone of the study is to celebrate a controversial life rather than to offer a more discursive interpretation of its implications. Its bibliography contains a helpful list of scholarly work on Malle, including American, French, Irish and German doctoral studies and shorter Masters' dissertations.

Braunschweig, M., and B. Gidel, *Les Déportés d'Avon. Enquête autour du film de Louis Malle, Au revoir les enfants* Paris: La Découverte, 1989. A moving account of the historical episode that lies behind *Au revoir les enfants*. Containing many extracts from primary historical sources this is a moving tribute to the victims of the Holocaust in France. Designed for use in French high schools, the book deserves a wider readership.

Chapier, Henry, *Louis Malle*, Paris, Seghers, 1964. This is the first critical study published on Malle. Its publication corresponded with the success of *Le Feu follet*. The book remains a valuable guide to Malle's early career and includes press dossiers of reviews of the early films.

de Santi, Gualterio, *Louis Malle*, Florence, Cinéma, 1977. A short study of Malle's work published in the 1970s. It is only available in the original Italian publication. Nevertheless, as with many other works listed here it is held at the British Film Institute Library, London.

Gitlin, Todd, 'Phantom India', *Film Quarterly* 27.4, 1974: 57–60. An extended review of Malle's major television documentary series. A helpful introduction.

Golsan, R. J., *Vichy's Afterlife: History and Counterhistory in Postwar France*, Lincoln NE, University of Nebraska Press, 2000. A collection of essays exploring France's troubled relationship with the Vichy period. Its second chapter offers an impassioned and highly accurate reading of *Lacombe Lucien*.

Hawkins, Peter, 1996 'Louis Malle: A European Outsider in the American Mainstream', in Wendy Everett (ed.) *European Identity in Cinema* (Bristol: Intellect), 30–4. A concise overview of Malle's work.

Higgins, Lynn, 'If Looks Could Kill: Louis Malle's Portraits of Collaboration', in Richard Golsan (ed.), *Fascism, Aesthetics and Culture*. Hanover: University Press of New England, 1989: 198–212. Probably the most persuasive account of how Malle's childhood came to haunt his later cinematic production. An important application of psychoanalytic film theory to Malle's work. Essential reading.

Kedward, H. R., '*Lacombe Lucien*: The Anti-Carnival of Collaboration', in Susan Hayward and Ginette Vincendeau (eds), *French Cinema: Texts and Contexts* London, Routledge, 2000. A prominent historian of the French resistance offers his interpretation of Malle's infamous film. The result is a success with Kedward showing a powerful understanding of Malle's work. The first edition of Hayward and Vincendeau's collection does not include this essay. It is a significant addition to the second edition.

Nicholls, David, 'Louis Malle's *Ascenseur pour l'échafaud* and the Presence of the Colonial Wars in French Cinema', *French Cultural Studies* 7, 1996: 271–82. A model of analysis of a film in its wider historical context.

Prédal, René, *Louis Malle*, Paris, Edilig, 1989. Malle's return to popularity in France with the release of *Au revoir les enfants* coincided with the publication of this major study. Prédal informs his readers that Malle commented on a draft of the monograph and so its content is of a quasi-critical, quasi-autobiographical nature. A major work on Mallean film that is especially strong when discussing Malle's technique of film-making.

Sellier, Geneviève and Ginette Vincendeau, 1998 'La Nouvelle Vague et le cinéma populaire: Brigitte Bardot dans *Vie privée* et *Le Mépris*', *Iris* 26, 1998: 115–29.

Sellier, Geneviève, 2001 'Gender, Modernism and Mass Culture in the New Wave', in Alex Hughes and James Williams (eds) *Gender and French Cinema* (Oxford: Berg): 125–37. Two important essays that explore the role of gender in New Wave cinema. Malle's *Vie privée* is discussed at some length and compared with Godard's treatment of Bardot in *Le Mépris*.

Index